HOW TO HEAR
THE LIVING WORD

HOW TO HEAR THE LIVING WORD

MARGARET PARKER

▼ VICTOR BOOKS
A DIVISION OF SCRIPTURE PRESS PUBLICATIONS INC.
USA CANADA ENGLAND

Most Scripture quotations are from the *Holy Bible, New International Version®*. Copyright © 1973, 1978, 1984 by International Bible Society. Used by permission of Zondervan Publishing House. All rights reserved. Other Scripture quotations are from *Good News Bible* (GNB) Old Testament: © American Bible Society 1976; New Testament: © American Bible Society 1966, 1971, 1976.

Editor: Carolyn Nystrom
Cover Design: Joe DeLeon
Cover Illustration: Frank McShane

Library of Congress Cataloging-in-Publication Data

Parker, Margaret, 1942–
   How to hear the living word / Margaret Parker.
     p. cm.
   ISBN 1-56476-270-X
   1. Bible as literature. 2. Christian life—1960– I. Title.
BS535.P285 1994
220.6'6—dc20   93-40252
                                                                              CIP

1   2   3   4   5   6   7   8   9   10   Printing/Year   98   97   96   95   94

© 1994 by Margaret Parker. All rights reserved. Printed in the United States of America. No part of this book may be reproduced without written permission, except for brief quotations in books, critical articles, and reviews.

VICTOR BOOKS
A division of SP Publications, Inc.
Wheaton, Illinois 60187

Contents

PREVIEW: What This Book Is All About 7

SESSION 1
Imagery: Stimulating Our Senses............................. 13

SESSION 2
Conflict: Getting Us Involved 19

SESSION 3
Tone: Touching Our Emotions................................ 26

SESSION 4
Contrast: Confronting Us with Choices 32

SESSION 5
Analogy: Gripping Our Imaginations 39

SESSION 6
Repetition: Making the Truth Sing 45

SESSION 7
Omission: Drawing Us into the Story 51

SESSION 8
Hyperbole: Exaggeration in the Service of Truth 60

SESSION 9
Poetic Justice: The Good Guys Win; The Bad Guys Lose 67

SESSION 10
Paradox: Beyond the Limits of Logic 75

SESSION 11
Dramatic Irony: We Know Something They Don't Know 83

SESSION 12
Echoes: Connecting Past, Present, and Future 91

WRAP-UP: Putting What You've Learned to Work 98

LEADER'S GUIDE: Introduction and Sessions 1–12 105

CHECKLIST OF LEARNING STRATEGIES 150

Preview

WHAT THIS BOOK IS ALL ABOUT

Remember Luke's picture of Martha's sister Mary sitting at Jesus' feet, totally absorbed in his teaching? I believe it would please our Lord if we opened the Bible this way, as if settling down at the feet of a wise and winsome friend. God wants us to become absorbed in the stories and enjoy the colorful language of Scripture. He wants us to make ourselves available to the Word, open ourselves to it. If we take the time to really get into the Bible, learning how to put our whole selves *into* our reading, God will enable us to get *out of* His Word just what He wants to give us.

The Bible is full of literary elements—elements like imagery and metaphor, conflict and contrast. These elements are designed to grab hold of us and draw us in. Learning how to follow literary paths into Scripture is what this book is all about.

WHY FOCUS ON LITERARY APPROACHES TO THE BIBLE?

If we believe that the Bible is the Word of God, learning how to read this book is one of the most important things we will ever do—for unless we can really hear what God is saying to us in His Word, we cannot respond in ways that please Him. One of the most effective ways to hear what God is saying is to become sensitive to the Bible's literary language. Unfortunately, many of us have never learned to tune in to the literary power of Scripture.

Many of us have learned to read the Bible as we would read a textbook or an instruction manual. We assume that the chief purpose of Scripture is to give us information about doctrine and history and ethics. Sometimes the Bible does speak to us in "informational" language that spells out theological concepts, or historical data, or guidelines for living. But more often we open our Bibles to find ourselves in a colorful and confusing landscape of lively stories, emotionally charged poetry, and pithy sayings. We have stepped outside the boundaries of orderly, logical communication and into the world of "literary" language where our textbook style of reading is not much help.

HOW TO HEAR THE LIVING WORD

How can we distinguish literary language from informational language? To answer that question, we will look at two brief passages from the epistles. In 2 Timothy 3:16-17, Paul tells us:

> All Scripture is inspired by God and profitable for teaching, for reproof, for correction, for training in righteousness; that the man of God may be adequate, equipped for every good work (NASB).

In Hebrews 4:12 we are told:

> The Word of God is alive and active, sharper than any double-edged sword. It cuts all the way through, to where soul and spirit meet, to where joints and marrow come together. It judges the desires and thoughts of man's heart (TEV).

Both these passages speak of the power that God's Word can have in our lives, but the kind of language they use is very different. The 2 Timothy passage is informational. It answers specific questions in an orderly fashion, and we can easily outline the ideas it teaches. Our outline might look like this:

I. *Where does Scripture come from?*
   It is inspired by God.

II. *What does Scripture accomplish?*
   It teaches, reproves, corrects, and trains us.

III. *Why do we read Scripture?*
   So that we will be people of God who are adequate and equipped for every good work.

The Hebrews passage is literary. Here God's Word is not the subject of abstract discussion, but a powerful living thing which we are forced to grapple with imaginatively. In our mind's eye we see Scripture, hard and bright as a carefully-honed sword, flashing dangerously as it closes in on us. We can feel the pain as the blade of God's truth slashes deep into the very heart of our being, exposing all our base desires, our ugly thoughts, the sins we have kept so well hidden from ourselves.

The 2 Timothy passage with its straightforward clarity works to inform our rational minds of the purpose and effectiveness of Scripture. In contrast, the Hebrews passage with its literary richness channels truth to us not only through our intellects, but through our senses, emotions, and imaginations as well. Fear, shame, and revulsion rise in us as we confront the prospect of our innermost beings cut open and spread out beneath the bright glare of God's Word.

Here we see demonstrated the principal difference between informational language and literary language. Informational language is reserved, careful language that tells us about something and allows us to deal with it intellectually. Literary language is aggressive language that reaches out to take hold of our whole beings so that we actually experience what is being talked about.

Because the Hebrews passage lets us experience the probing, purifying power God intends his Word to have in our lives, it forces us to ask ourselves, "Is the living, active Word described here like the Bible I know?" We will probably have to answer that the Bible we read often seems tame and ineffectual by comparison.

Our failure to experience the full power of Scripture may be due in large part to the fact that our reading is essentially a studious search for answers to doctrinal, historical, and ethical questions. We need to learn new styles of reading that involve our feelings and imaginations, styles that can mine the riches of the literary language in the Bible.

We will not want to abandon our information-seeking approaches to Bible study. God's Word includes both informational and literary language, and most passages are neither purely literary nor purely informational, but combine elements of both. Nevertheless, far more biblical language belongs at the literary end of the spectrum than at the informational. That is why this book focuses on literary approaches to Scripture.

HOW IS THIS BOOK STRUCTURED?

Each of the twelve sessions in this book focuses on a different literary element and lets the user practice ways to pursue that element into Scripture. The first three parts of each session make up a well-rounded small group study. All sessions include the following four parts:

1. An *Introduction* to the literary element being highlighted explains how this element works in Scripture to enable God's message to take hold of us.
2. A brief exercise called *Tuning In* helps people feel comfortable with the literary element—even if they are not "literary" types.
3. The *Pursuing* section, a study of a single Bible passage or closely related passages, demonstrates how the literary element can work to draw participants into Scripture so they can experience its meaning in fresh ways.
4. A final section called *Further Exploration* is not intended to be part of the group study. This section gives individuals the chance to practice additional ways to focus on the literary element in different kinds of biblical literature.

The *Wrap-up* that follows the twelve sessions explains how the various literary elements and learning strategies presented in this book can be applied to future Bible study or teaching.

A *Leader's Guide* rounds out the book. Whether you are studying the book individually, leading a small group through it, or using it as a resource in a class, you will find helpful pointers and suggested answers in this section. You will enjoy the book more and learn more from it, however, if you work through the exercises yourself before consulting the Leader's Guide.

A *Checklist of Learning Strategies* appears at the end of the book. This list indexes the approaches demonstrated throughout these twelve sessions. With it you can mix and match strategies to fit personal study tastes as you look at any biblical text.

WHO CAN BENEFIT FROM THIS BOOK?

How to Hear the Living Word is written especially with leaders of small group Bible studies in mind. If you are a small group facilitator, you have much to gain from learning how to pursue literary approaches to Scripture.

First, as you pursue literary paths you will find that you read the Bible with more pleasure and you will feel its words hitting home more often. The new enjoyment and excitement you experience in studying God's Word will be conveyed to your group. Second, as you employ literary approaches in group discussions, members will be learning how to read the Bible better for themselves. Finally, following literary paths into Scripture together will enhance the dynamics of your group. As people share their emotional and imaginative responses to God's Word, they will be sharing very personal values, feelings, and experiences in a nonthreatening way that strengthens and deepens the bonds in the group.

But this book is not solely for facilitators and their groups. Anyone who wants to learn to read or teach Scripture more effectively can benefit from these guided studies.

WHAT ARE SOME WAYS TO USE THIS BOOK?

Individuals, small groups, or larger classes can all use *How to Hear the Living Word.*

- Individuals can work their way through the book, choosing to do the sessions in any order and at any pace that suits them.
- A small group can study this book, covering one session at each meeting. The group may choose to do only the first six sessions (which introduce the most essential literary elements), or it may add any of the other sessions that are of interest. Each chapter offers optional exercises for groups that spend an extended time together.
- A class on "How to Read the Bible" can use this book as a resource, focusing on selected materials and exercises to demonstrate how helpful it is to become sensitive to the literary elements in Scripture.

In addition, *How to Hear the Living Word* lends itself to formal training of small group leaders or Bible teachers. Here are some ways that might work:

- If leaders or teachers meet weekly or monthly in their own small group, they can work their way through the sessions as any small group would.
- Several of the sessions can be presented together in an intensive training workshop or leaders' retreat.
- Individual exercises from this book can be inserted into other planning or training sessions to stimulate participants to try new approaches to Bible study and teaching.

This book teaches a wide range of learning strategies. Some are quite left-brained and analytical. You'll do things like make lists and fill in charts as you seek to tune in to some of the literary elements in God's Word. But more imaginative approaches are particularly helpful when we are trying to enter with our whole beings into the truths God wants us to experience. Therefore, you'll also find yourself doing such things as recalling childhood memories, drawing cartoons, and dialoguing with Jesus.

Because the literary paths this book teaches blend studious attention with a playful openness to the Word, following these paths is more like an adventure than an assignment. Each session is a journey of intellect, imagination, and faith. Are you ready to begin?

1

IMAGERY
Stimulating Our Senses

Isaiah 6:1-8

INTRODUCTION

One of the best ways to make a lasting impression on people, to change their attitudes or their behavior, is to approach their minds and hearts through their senses. Driver-education teachers who want their students to obey speed limits and seat-belt laws show them gory films of actual accidents, with ambulance sirens on the soundtrack and mangled bodies on the screen. Hunger relief organizations anxious to collect contributions place magazine ads showcasing children with arms like sticks and bellies like melons and flies crawling over their fragile bodies. Auto companies wooing people to buy their new sports car show a commercial with a red model swooping around the curves of a scenic cliff while waves crash below and upbeat music soars in the background.

We learn through our senses. From the time we are born, they connect us with the world. The toys in a crib teach us about color and texture, the foods we eat teach us about smell and taste, the voices that speak to us teach us about language, and the hands that touch us teach us about love. Though our minds later develop the ability to handle abstract ideas, we never outgrow our appetites for sensory input.

Effective teachers understand that the more they get people's senses involved, the greater impact they will make. That is why they use audiovisual aids, pace back and forth in front of the class, and dramatize their subject through tones of voice and gestures. Writers, like teachers, hope to make an impact, but they are not present with their audience. How can they connect with people's senses? Writers use imagery.

Imagery is language that suggests sights or sounds, tastes or smells, textures or internal feelings. This language stimulates our imaginations to recreate what is being described. We have the wonderful capacity to picture the images we read "in our mind's eye," hear them "in our mind's ear," or even smell them "in our mind's nose."

God wants His Word to make a long-term, life-changing impression on us, so naturally the Bible is full of imagery. Unfortunately, the images too often slip right by us. As members of the TV generation, we have forgotten how to respond to such language. Since the pictures, voices, sound effects, and laugh track of the "tube" do most of the work our imaginations were designed to do, our imaginative muscles have grown flabby. But by making the effort to tune in to the powerful imagery in Scripture, we can exercise these muscles and reactivate our imaginations. God is waiting to touch our minds and hearts through this sensuous language.

TUNING IN
to Imagery

Which of your senses, other than sight, do you think is most acute? Are you more attuned to sound, smell, taste, or touch stimuli? Or are you more sensitive to internal sensations like pain, hunger, or fatigue? Give examples.

IMAGERY

PURSUING
Imagery in Isaiah 6:1-8

1. You may equate imagery with highly descriptive language that uses lots of adjectives and adverbs. The passages in this session, however, appeal to our senses mainly through strong, straightforward nouns and verbs. Such words suggest concrete experiences but leave room for our imaginations to fill in the details.

Read Isaiah 6:1-8, a description of how Isaiah experienced God's call to him. This passage appeals to several senses. As you focus your imagination on its imagery, what do you . . .

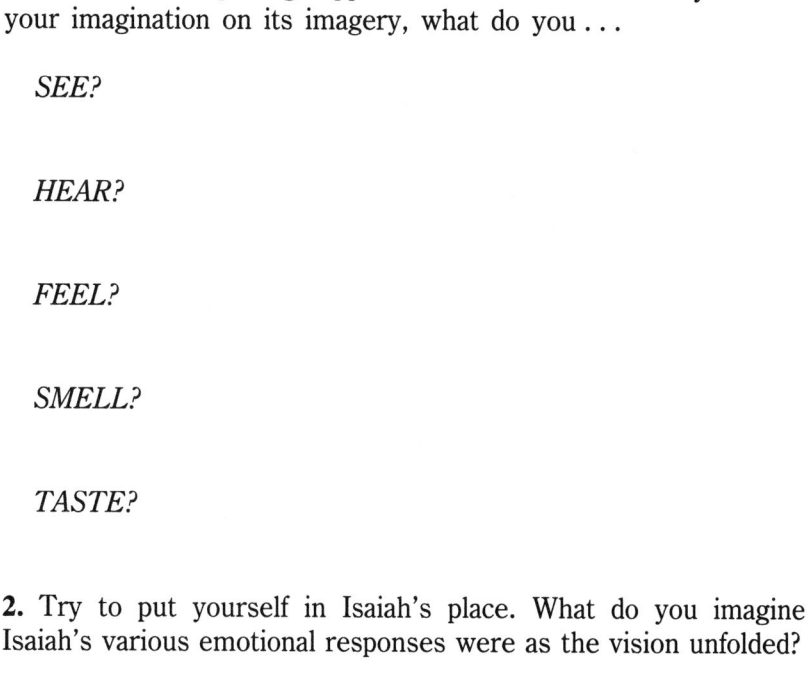

SEE?

HEAR?

FEEL?

SMELL?

TASTE?

2. Try to put yourself in Isaiah's place. What do you imagine Isaiah's various emotional responses were as the vision unfolded?

3. What effect do you think this experience had on the rest of Isaiah's life? Why?

HOW TO HEAR THE LIVING WORD

4. Recall a time when God reached out to you in a way that changed your life. To what extent did He work through your senses to touch your mind and heart? Give specific examples of things God gave you to see, hear, feel, taste, or smell that made a lasting impression on you.

5. While God sometimes reaches out in dramatic ways to touch our lives, He also is present for us on a day-to-day basis. What is one way God has reached out to touch you in the last day or two, making His presence known through your senses?

6. Isaiah 6:9-10 sounds a warning. Our eyes may be closed and our ears dulled so that we cannot hear and see God. What things tend to get in the way of you experiencing God in your daily life?

7. What do you think you could do to keep yourself more open and sensitive to God's presence?

IMAGERY

FURTHER EXPLORATION
of Imagery in Scripture

Exercise 1 — **Ephesians 3:16-19**
A. Some biblical images have become so familiar to us that we forget they can appeal to our senses and imaginations. In Ephesians 3:17 Paul prays for those he is writing to "that Christ may dwell in [their] hearts through faith." Has having Christ in your heart become a cliché for you? Try opening your senses to this image. What picture comes to your mind when you think of Christ dwelling in your heart?

B. Paul's prayer in Ephesians 3:16-19 contains several other suggestive images:

- "out of His glorious riches He may strengthen you" (v. 16)
- "being rooted and established in love" (v. 17)
- "grasp how wide and long and high and deep is the love of Christ" (v. 18)
- "you may be filled to the measure of all the fullness of God" (v. 19)

Read Ephesians 3:16-19. Choose the two images above that particularly appeal to your imagination. Then draw a picture or write a descriptive paragraph to represent the picture that each of the phrases suggests to you.

HOW TO HEAR THE LIVING WORD

C. Having put yourself imaginatively into the images of Ephesians 3:16-19, read the passage again, praying it as your own personal prayer.

Exercise 2—**Amos 6:1, 4-7**
A. Images that grow out of the culture of Bible times may speak more forcefully to us if we "translate" them into our current setting. Read Amos 6:1, 4-7 and rewrite it so the images fit our culture. You might begin, "Woe to you who are complacent in America... you stretch out in your recliners, watching TV."

B. Of all the images of comfort and luxury in Amos 6:1, 4-7, which speaks loudest to you personally? Why?

C. Verse 6 suggests that in the midst of material comforts we can be blind to ruin around or within us. "Ruin" is a powerful word. If you apply it to contemporary society, what images does it call up?

D. How sensitive are you to the contemporary "ruins" you listed above?

2

CONFLICT
Getting Us Involved

Luke 9:46-50

INTRODUCTION

Conflict equals drama—and drama equals entertainment. When we are in the mood to be entertained, we usually seek out conflict in some form. Think of the sports we watch, the games we play, the movies we see, the books we read. Inevitably they revolve around competition and conflict. Whether the clash is between friendly rivals or deadly enemies, we find our emotions gripped by the drama of confrontation, and we don't feel satisfied until we see the outcome of the contest.

Since conflict has this power to get us involved, one of the best ways to enter into many Bible passages is to look first for the conflicts in them. These conflicts may come in many shapes and sizes. There are individual internal struggles, clashes between personalities, and antagonisms between social or national groups. Various ideas or values can be at war with each other. Often in Scripture we see spiritual conflicts between humans and God, and sometimes the cosmic conflict between God and Satan.

HOW TO HEAR THE LIVING WORD

A complex web of conflicts may operate in a single passage. The Garden of Gethsemane before Jesus' crucifixion was the scene of several confrontations. Jesus wrestled in prayer with His own fears (internal conflict) and with God's will (spiritual conflict). He also confronted His disciples because they could not stay awake to watch and pray with Him (interpersonal conflict). The disciples experienced a struggle between their physical exhaustion and their desire to support Jesus (internal conflict). When the soldiers came to arrest Jesus, one of His disciples attacked the chief priest's servant, cutting off his ear (conflict between different groups). Then Jesus opposed that disciple's use of violence, saying it was time to surrender to God's will, not to fight (conflicting values or motivations). These conflicts, coming one on top of the other, make the story of Gethsemane both poignant and gripping.

Though the idea may sound surprising, even sacrilegious, reading the Bible can be entertaining. Since the dramatic confrontations in its pages invite emotional involvement, let's let ourselves get involved. Surely God will be pleased if we find His Word as exciting as a football game or as moving as a novel. When we allow the conflicts in the Bible to take hold of us, we are learning to care about the things that matter to God.

TUNING IN
to Conflict

When was the last time you chose a form of recreation or entertainment that involved some kind of conflict? Describe this activity, and explain why it appealed to you.

PURSUING
Conflict in Luke 9:46-50

1. The NIV Bible titles Luke 9:46-50 "Who Will Be the Greatest?" This brief passage may seem rather bland, even "preachy," until

CONFLICT

we pay attention to the conflicts that are operating in it. Read this passage through two or three times. How many conflicts are mentioned here? Who comes into conflict with whom? What motivates these confrontations?

2. Define the most fundamental conflict in this passage, the one between Jesus and His disciples. What does Jesus represent here? What do His disciples represent?

3. Imagine that there are two teams pitted against each other. On one team are those who follow Jesus' teaching in this passage. On the other team are those who act as His disciples acted. These two teams represent two different ways to play "the game of life." Do the following:

- Name each team, choosing a name that captures the essence of what each stands for. (Jesus' team might be called the "Givers," and the opposing team might be called the "Grabbers.")

- Think up a slogan or motto for each team.

- List the basic strategies that each team uses in the game of life. You will find some ideas in the passage itself—for example, the disciples flaunt their membership in the "in group." But you may come up with additional strategies not specifically demonstrated in the passage.

- List the qualifications a person must have in order to belong to each team.

- If you were a scout for each team, name three people (well-known personalities in history or our current world) that you would be anxious to recruit.

4. Note that the people Jesus came in conflict with in Luke 9:46-50 were His own disciples. Similarly, even though we are followers of Jesus, we often slip into attitudes and ways of behaving that do not please our Lord. Is there a particular setting, or relationship, or activity where you are prone to demonstrate the same kind of competitiveness that the disciples were displaying? Explain.

CONFLICT

5. Imagine Jesus here in the flesh to witness your behavior the next time you get caught up in a typical episode of competitiveness. What do you think He would say to you? (You may want to paraphrase Luke 9:48, or imagine words that are directed more specifically to your own situation.)

6. How would you want to respond to Christ's words? Write your response as a prayer.

FURTHER EXPLORATION
of Conflict in Scripture

Exercise 1 — **Psalm 73**
A. Read Psalm 73 aloud. List all the internal conflicts the psalmist is struggling with in this psalm.

B. Do you ever struggle with similar conflicts? Explain.

C. In what ways are the conflicts in the psalm resolved?

If you have ever experienced a similar resolution for your internal struggles, write down your memories of that experience.

D. Which verses in the psalm speak special comfort to you? Write them down and put them somewhere where you will see them often. You may want to memorize these verses.

Exercise 2—**Genesis 29:16–30:24**
A. Read Genesis 29:16–30:24, which portrays a personal conflict between two sisters. What are the roots of this conflict?

CONFLICT

B. Develop character sketches of these two sisters. Fill in enough detail so that they come alive for you.

C. How do you think God wants us to handle conflicts that seem as deep and resistant to healing as this one between Rachel and Leah? If these two women came to you for counseling, how would you counsel them to deal with their conflict?

3

TONE
Touching Our Emotions

Hosea 11:1-11

INTRODUCTION

Remember as a child, how much you were affected by your parents' tones of voice? When you brought home a painting from school, did your mother proclaim "That's beautiful!" before she put it up on the refrigerator, or did she mumble a preoccupied "That's nice, Honey"? When you were afraid of the dark, was your father's tone sympathetic as he tucked you in, or did his "Good night" have an impatient edge that said your fears were silly? If you misbehaved, did Mom or Dad say "Don't do that" in a plaintive voice that told you you didn't really have to mind, or was their tone so authoritative that you knew you'd better shape up?

We learn early that people communicate with more than words. Their tones, their expressions, their gestures all help to get their points across. Tone of voice is often the best clue to the emotion that lies behind a spoken message. We tune in to tone to find out what a person is really trying to say and how we can respond appropriately.

TONE

The same principle applies when we read God's Word. The Bible is personal communication—God speaking to us through the voices of people in history. Its pages are packed with emotion. We'll miss much of its meaning if we read the printed text without listening for the tone that tells us the feelings behind the words.

It's easy to catch the tone of voice in many parts of Scripture. The psalmists' feelings come through loud and clear, whether they are complaining to God or praising Him. The prophets use highly emotional language too. Sometimes they express their own feelings, but often we hear God Himself pouring out His heart through their writings. And in the Epistles, which were written to instruct, inspire, warn, and encourage the early Christians, we can often hear the deep feelings which Paul, James, Peter, and John had for their brothers and sisters in Christ.

The narrative passages in the Bible have their own tone, though it may not be as easy for us to hear. Bible stories seldom mention emotions explicitly, concentrating on action and dialogue instead. Nevertheless, if we read carefully we can usually imagine how the voices in dialogue would sound, and we can catch the mood of the action and the writer's attitude toward it.

Beneath all the other voices in Scripture, we can hear God's voice. As God's children, we need to listen not only with our minds but with our hearts when our Heavenly Father speaks. One of the best ways we can open our hearts to what God is saying to us is to listen for tone as we read His Word.

TUNING IN
to Tone

Recall one tone of voice that you particularly remember your father or your mother using. What situation would call forth this tone? How did hearing it affect you?

HOW TO HEAR THE LIVING WORD

PURSUING
Tone in Hosea 11:1-11

1. In this passage, God is speaking about His chosen people Israel (also called "Ephraim") as if they were His child. God's words are packed with emotion. As you read Hosea 11:1-11, jot here or in the margin the tones of voice you hear, and note where you hear them changing.

Read through the passage again and imagine the gestures or facial expressions that might accompany God's words. Jot down phrases to describe these gestures and expressions.

2. How do you react personally to the passionate, changeable feelings God expresses here? Does anything in these verses surprise you? Delight you? Confuse you? Frighten you? Reassure you? Explain.

3. How would you describe God's nature, based on these verses?

4. God saw the Israelites whom He loved defying Him and making foolish choices that would lead to destructive consequences. Is

TONE

someone you love making foolish choices? What are your feelings toward that person?

Which of your feelings toward that person are similar to the ones God expresses in Hosea 11:1-11? Which are different?

5. Imagine God speaking specifically about the person you pinpointed in Question 4. Using Hosea 11:1-11 as a model, write down the words you think God might say, the feelings He might express, about that person's past, present, and future. Begin with, "When _____ was a child, I loved him, and . . . ." If you need more space, use a separate sheet of paper.

6. Having done the preceding exercise, do you feel God may be calling you to change your attitudes toward this person, the way you interact with him or her, or the way you pray? Describe the changes you think God might want you to make.

FURTHER EXPLORATION
of Tone in Scripture

Exercise 1 — **Acts 9:1-19**
A. Read Acts 9:1-19, which tells about Saul's conversion. Imagine that you are dramatizing this scene for radio. There will be four voices: the Narrator, the Lord Jesus, Saul, and Ananias. How do you think the various lines should be read to best convey the feeling in the passage? Read the passage out loud, trying to put the appropriate tone and expression into your voice.

B. There is considerable room for different interpretations in guessing the tone of voice in some passages. In what different ways might Jesus have said, "Saul, Saul, why are you persecuting Me?"

What tone do you think Jesus probably used? What does your guess say about how you see Jesus?

TONE

Exercise 2—**1 Samuel 31:1-13 and 2 Samuel 1:19-27**
A. Background music often contributes enormously to the drama in a movie. Do you have a favorite movie soundtrack? What is it? What makes it memorable for you? Why?

B. By imagining background music to biblical narratives or poetry, we can heighten the impact that the words have on us. Read aloud 1 Samuel 31:1-13 (a narrative about Saul's death) and 2 Samuel 1:19-27 (David's lament for Saul and Jonathan). What background music would you choose to accompany these passages? What instruments, what beat, what kind of melody would best help to convey the action and emotions? (The tone might stay the same throughout, or it might shift from one paragraph or stanza to the next.)

C. We are hearing the words of a history writer in 1 Samuel 31:1-13, and in 2 Samuel 1:19-27 that writer is quoting the words of David. But behind these historical speakers, can you also hear God's voice, God's heart in these passages? Explain.

4

CONTRAST
Confronting Us with Choices

Ephesians 2:1-10

INTRODUCTION

Probably you've seen a cold-remedy commercial like this: A couple lies in bed in the middle of the night. The husband slumps against his pillow, eyes wide open, nose running, body racked by uncontrollable coughing. Beside him, in striking contrast, his wife slumbers peacefully. He shakes her awake, demanding "How can you sleep with your cold? I haven't gotten a wink all night." She points to the bottle of night-time cold medicine on her bedside table before falling again into blissful oblivion.

Advertisers often employ contrasts like this. Why? Because striking contrasts capture our attention. They show us clearly the options that are available to us and persuade us to choose one option over another. They sell the product.

We should not be surprised to find contrast used frequently in Scripture. After all, God's Word is in a sense divine advertising. God wants to persuade us to abandon our sinful ways and buy into abundant life with Him. He has inspired the biblical writers to present vivid contrasts—light vs. darkness, life vs. death, love vs. alienation—to highlight the crucial choices before us and help us choose rightly.

Think how many contrasts operate in Jesus' Parable of the Prodigal Son. There is the grasping attitude of the younger son vs. the generosity of the father; the prodigal's cocksure self-sufficiency when he leaves home vs. his abject sense of neediness when he returns; the illusory, short-lived pleasure of partying in the far country vs. the solid joy of celebrating at home; the father's exuberant reception of the returning prodigal vs. the brother's bitter resentment toward him; the elder son's insistence on getting what he deserves vs. the younger son's willingness to receive love freely given. Each contrast can touch us at a different point in our lives and teach us a different lesson. All the contrasts working together give this parable great power to propel us into the arms of our waiting Father or to compel us to forgive our wayward brother.

Our society is constantly bombarding us with insistent messages that the ways of the world—false gods, flimsy values, fleeting pleasures—are the way to happiness. The choices we face are bewildering. But if we focus our attention on the contrasts God paints in Scripture, these contrasts will forcefully remind us that the life our Lord offers is incomparably better than anything the world wants to sell us.

TUNING IN
to Contrast

How many commercials or advertisements can you think of that use contrast to sell a product or service? List them.

PURSUING
Contrast in Ephesians 2:1-10

1. Ephesians 2:1-10 serves as a forceful advertisement for the faith. In it Paul asks us to consider the differences between life with Christ and life without Christ. Read the passage through two or three times. (You may want to use different versions of the Bible, because one may paint a particular contrast more clearly than another does.) On the chart below, fill in all the contrasts you can find between life without Christ and life with Christ.

LIFE WITHOUT CHRIST VS.	LIFE WITH CHRIST

2. Take some time to meditate on the different word pictures Paul uses to highlight the contrasts between life without Christ and life with Christ. What do these pictures make you think of, see, feel? For example, when you read the phrase "dead in your transgressions," do you visualize someone laid out in a mortuary, or decaying in a grave? When you think of being seated with Christ "in the heavenly realms," what setting do you imagine? Let your mind play with both the negative and positive word pictures Paul draws until you sense their full emotional impact.

Which contrast in the passage hits you hardest? Write down the ideas, the pictures, the feelings Paul's words produce in your mind

CONTRAST

and heart. Why does this contrast speak forcefully to you?

3. Paul's commercial in Ephesians 2:1-10 is essentially a "before and after" appeal, drawing general contrasts between what life is like for people before they choose Christ and what it is like after conversion. (Such "before and after" testimonials are used often in advertising—for example, to sell diet programs.) Think of as many contrasts as you can between your life now and your life before you knew Christ. Jot down these contrasts. (If you cannot remember a time when you did not believe in Christ, then write down contrasts between a period when you were distant from God and a time when you drew close to Him again.)

4. Pick out one of the contrasts you listed in Question 3. Write a "before and after" testimonial built around that contrast. Use an anecdote or word picture that portrays your own experience in a way you think would appeal to people who are not believers. (This doesn't need to be polished writing. Just put down whatever ideas God gives you.)

5. Can you remember a time when you shared a "before and after" testimonial like this with either a believer or a nonbeliever? What was his/her reaction?

Do you think there is value in sharing your testimony with someone who already knows Christ? Why or why not?

Think of someone you know who is not a believer. How do you think that person would react to hearing the testimonial you have just written?

6. Take this chance to speak to God and thank Him for the changes He has made in your life. Ask Him for opportunities, courage, and sensitivity to share your experiences with others so they, too, will be drawn to the Savior. (You may want to write out your prayer here.)

CONTRAST

FURTHER EXPLORATION
of Contrast in Scripture

Exercise 1 — Psalm 1
A. Read Psalm 1 aloud. What contrasting images are used in verses 3-4? Draw a picture or pictures to express how you experience these contrasting images.

B. What choice does the psalmist want his readers to make?

C. Do you think the contrasting images the psalmist chooses are powerful and persuasive in selling his idea to a modern audience? Why or why not?

Exercise 2 — Isaiah 46:1-7
A. Read Isaiah 46:1-7. The preceding chapter, Isaiah 45, has been speaking about how God will rescue His people from exile in Babylon by raising up Cyrus to overthrow the Babylonians. Now in Isaiah 46:1-2, the prophet describes how the Babylonians will try to escape with their idols but will be captured. In verses 3-7 God

speaks to His people in exile, reassuring them that their captors, who seem so powerful, are really pathetic because they trust in idols, whereas the Israelites are blessed because they have a relationship with the living God.

List below all the contrasts you find in verses 1–7. (Look for ways that God is different from false gods, and for contrasts between the benefits that God's prople enjoy and the disappointments that idol worshipers suffer.)

B. In our culture today we do not bow down to statues of wood or metal or stone, yet there are things we do put our trust in which are really as powerless to save as the idols of the Babylonians. What are various false gods that are worshiped in our culture?

C. Which one of these current false gods has the most powerful hold over the people you know? Compose an oracle as if God were condemning this particular idol. With Isaiah 46:1-7 as a model, use contrasts to emphasize how foolish people are to worship this false god when they could be worshiping the real God.

5

ANALOGY
Gripping Our Imaginations

Hebrews 12:1-13

INTRODUCTION

When we are trying to convey what we think or feel about something, we often compare it with something else that is in most ways quite different from it. "My geology exam was a picnic," we say. Or, "It looks like she poured herself into that dress." Or, "That new employee works like a beaver." Our words are literally nonsense. Geology exams don't include sandwiches and potato salad. A woman's body is solid flesh, not liquid. And employees do not gnaw down trees. Yet all these phrases manage to communicate; and even though they are clichés, they remind us how colorful and effective analogies between unlike things can be.

The Bible is full of colorful analogies. A familiar example is Psalm 23, which compares God to a shepherd and His people to sheep. Actually the term "analogy" can refer to a number of closely related literary strategies, including simile, metaphor, and parable. A simile states explicitly that one thing is like another, as when Isaiah says, "All we, like sheep, have gone astray." A metaphor identifies one thing with another, as in, "The Lord is my shepherd." A parable gives us a story of an earthly circumstance that parallels some deeper truth. For example, when Jesus tells about the shepherd who leaves his whole flock to find one lost sheep, He demonstrates God's determination to rescue every lost soul.

By making striking, often unexpected connections between unlike things, analogies grip our imaginations. When we meet an analogy, our job is not to try to translate it immediately into an abstract principle or doctrine, but to let our imaginations play with it until we experience its power for us personally. When we read Isaiah's words, "All we, like sheep, have gone astray," we miss the impact of the simile if we just respond, "Of course, all humans sin." Instead we should begin to wonder: *Am I like a sheep? When and where have I strayed?*

It's important to remember that similes, metaphors, and parables are not just some fancy wrapping God puts around what He wants to say. They are the best way, perhaps the only way, He can convey what He means. For sometimes what God wants to tell us is beyond our human understanding. We could not begin to comprehend the Lord's loving care for us if the Bible did not convey that care in pictures that are within the realm of our human experience—pictures of fathers and shepherds. At other times what God wants to tell us is repugnant to our rebellious natures. We don't want to hear that we are sinful. But the truth of our waywardness may penetrate our defenses when Isaiah clothes that truth in a simile about sheep which will appeal to our imagination.

Of course, no single analogy in Scripture can capture truth pure and whole. We humans are like sheep in some ways, but in many other ways we are nothing like sheep. God may be our shepherd, but He is also king, gardener, judge, husband, potter, fortress, lion—the list goes on and on. It is only as we explore the rich variety of metaphors in the Bible and see how they complement and illuminate one another that we can experience their full power. The more sensitive we become to biblical analogies, the more grateful we will grow for them. Many painful and beautiful truths God wants to teach us could not touch us deeply if they were not wrapped up in concrete, down-to-earth analogies.

ANALOGY

**TUNING IN
to Analogy**

Think of an analogy you would use to describe either your home life or your job. For example, if you live with a large family whose members are always coming and going, you might say your home is like Grand Central Station; if you work hard at your job but have no hope of advancement, you might describe that job as an endless ride on a stationary bicycle.

**PURSUING
Analogy in Hebrews 12:1-13**

1. One of the underlying purposes of the Book of Hebrews is to strengthen Christians in their faith when they are suffering hardship or persecution. Hebrews 12:1-13 uses two basic analogies to encourage people to remain faithful to God in the face of difficulties. Read aloud Hebrews 12:1-13. (The "great cloud of witnesses" referred to in verse 1 represents all those Old Testament saints described in Hebrews 11 who held on to their faith through great trials.)

Now reread verses 1-3, where the central metaphor compares keeping the faith to running a race. How many ways can you think of in which Christians are like athletes and keeping the faith is like a race?

2. What role do you see Jesus playing in this sports metaphor?

41

3. Why would this sports analogy motivate people to hold to their faith when they were being tested by persecution or hardship?

4. Hebrews 12:4-11 switches to a family analogy, saying that when a Christian endures hardships, it is like a child experiencing a father's discipline. Read Hebrews 12:4-11.

What memories do you have of a father's discipline from your own childhood? (If you did not have a father present, was there someone else who exercised parental discipline in your life?)

5. Do your memories help you respond to the metaphor of a loving God who disciplines His children? Or do your childhood experiences make it difficult for you to relate to the picture of God in Hebrews 12:5-11? Explain.

6. Which of the metaphors—running a race or parental discipline—is most inspiring for you? Why?

7. Think of someone you care about who is experiencing circumstances that make it hard to hold on to faith. Write a "pep talk" for that person similar to the one you have just read in Hebrews 12:1-13.

ANALOGY

But choose as your central metaphor something that you think would be especially meaningful for your friend. (You might choose another kind of sports analogy, for example, if your friend is involved in a sport other than running. Or if your friend is a gardener, you might compare hardships he/she is facing to the processes of weeding, pruning, and fertilizing that God is using to stimulate growth in your friend's faith.)

8. If you feel your friend would gain encouragement right now from the word picture you thought of, why not send a note and share it with your friend?

FURTHER EXPLORATION
of Analogy in Scripture

Exercise 1 — **Philippians 2:14-16**
A. Read Philippians 2:14-16. This passage says Christians can shine like stars if, instead of complaining and arguing, they hold out the Word of Life in a crooked and depraved generation. List all the similarities you can think of between joyful Christians and shining stars.

B. Think of a particular situation or relationship in your life where you believe you do "shine like a star" sometimes. Briefly describe this situation and the role you play in it.

C. Think of a particular situation or relationship in your life where you do not "shine like a star," but instead tend to argue and complain a lot. Now think of a metaphor for how you act in that situation and write it here. "Rather than shining like a star, I . . .

D. What value do you see in defining your negative behavior in terms of a word picture like the one you just made up?

Exercise 2—**Matthew 7:1-5**
A. The word *parable* comes from a Greek word that means "putting things side by side," and most parables are also analogies. Read Matthew 7:1-5, Jesus' Parable of the Log and the Splinter. How is the picture this parable presents analogous to something that happens often in the course of our relationships with others?

B. The Parable of the Log and Splinter is similar to a comedy sketch on TV that evokes laughter by exaggerating our all-too-human weaknesses. Write your own brief comedy sketch that uses a contemporary situation to make the same point as Christ's Parable of the Log and Splinter.

6

REPETITION
Making the Truth Sing

Daniel 3:1-30

INTRODUCTION

Much of life is repetition. Our hearts beat steadily, night and day follow each other endlessly, the seasons come around again and again. As if these natural cycles are not enough to satisfy us, we make up countless rituals of our own and adhere to them religiously. We go through the same routines on arising each morning, look forward to the same TV programs each week, repeat the same holiday traditions each year.

Repetition is everywhere in Scripture. Most of us recognize it in the Psalms, where the same idea is often stated in different ways in succeeding verses. But there are countless other places in the Bible where repetition is used to good effect. Think of all the echoes in the account of Creation in Genesis 1. Over and over we hear:

"And God said, 'Let there be....' And it was so."
"And God saw that it was good."
"And there was evening, and there was morning"

These repeated phrases create in us not boredom but a profound sense of order, of unwavering purpose and inexhaustible power, of grand achievement and vast satisfaction.

Repetition in Scripture impacts us in various ways. It's often used to underline what is really important, as if warning us, "If you don't remember anything else, remember this!" Thus the phrases that echo through Genesis 1 leave no question in our minds that God created everything in the world and that everything He created is good. Furthermore, the very rhythm established by repetition sometimes reflects the particular message of a passage; thus the orderly building of paragraph on paragraph in Genesis 1 reflects the orderly universe that God has created. Repetition is useful too because when a pattern is broken, the surprise brings us up short, riveting our attention. When we come to the creation of man in Genesis 1:26, God's words are not "Let there be . . . ," but "Let Us make man in Our image, in Our likeness." We immediately sense that human beings are a different order of creation.

Beyond recognizing the many ways that repetition may reinforce the meaning of a particular passage, we should remember that it is, quite simply, a source of pleasure. From our youngest days of listening to nonsense rhymes ("This little pig went to market, this little pig stayed home. . . ."), we delight in the rhythm of sounds. Songs which combine a regular beat, a repeated melody, and the predictability of lyrics in a chorus have particular power to move us. It is as if they connect with something essential in us, harmonizing with the regular tide of our breathing and the pulsing of blood in our veins.

To better hear the rhythms of Scripture, we probably need to read passages out loud. As we catch the beat of the words, the phrases that recur like choruses, the themes that echo through the verses, our reading will be more enjoyable. God's Word can become "music to our ears."

TUNING IN
to Repetition

What is one of your favorite hymns or worship songs? As you recite or sing the song, note the repetitions in words and/or melody.

REPETITION

PURSUING
Repetition in Daniel 3:1-30

1. The account of Shadrach, Meshach, and Abednego in the fiery furnace is one of the most dramatic stories in the Bible, a wonderful story of faith and God's faithfulness. First read Daniel 1:1–2:1 and 2:25-28, 46-49 so you will understand how these three Jewish exiles came to occupy high positions in the government of their conqueror, King Nebuchadnezzar of Babylon.

Read Daniel 3:1-30 out loud. Simply relax and enjoy the passage, trying to listen as if you are hearing it for the first time. You can't miss the repetitions in this story. What are some examples?

2. In verses 1-15, underline the places where it is mentioned that King Nebuchadnezzar has "set up" the image of gold. Then circle the places where the commanded response of "falling down and worshiping" the image is described. How do these repetitions serve to underline what the king is really asking his subjects to do?

3. Repetitions can be used to give us insights into the character of people. In verses 1-15, a long list of officials whom the king commands to worship the image of gold is repeated, as is a long list of instruments which are to be played. How do these repetitions of the king's commands help give you a picture of the king? What kind of picture do they give?

Read verses 16-18, the reply of Shadrach, Meshach, and Abednego to the king's commands. Their response contains no repetitions.

What picture of the character of these three men does their speech give you? How does this contrast with the picture you formed of the king?

4. There is lots of suspense in Daniel 3, and the repeated mention of being thrown into a blazing furnace in verses 6, 11, 15, 17, and 20-21 contributes to this suspense. If you had never read this narrative before, and stopped at verse 23, how do you think you would have guessed that the story would end?

What about the way the story *does* end takes you by surprise? Why?

5. In verses 12-23, how often are the names Shadrach, Meshach, and Abednego repeated?

There is pleasure in hearing the sound of these three musical names over and over. But beyond this, how does the repetition of the names contribute to the powerful turning point of the story found in verses 24-26?

How does it contribute to the lesson the story teaches?

REPETITION

6. This is a story about faithfulness to God. How would you describe the faith of Shadrach, Meshach, and Abednego?

7. Do you feel that the kind of faith these three displayed would be impossible for you? Can you remember situations where you have hidden or denied your faith in much less threatening circumstances?

Write a personal dialogue with God around this question of faith. You might begin, "Lord, I don't think I could stand up for You as Shadrach, Meshach, and Abednego did." God might reply, "Why is that, My child?" Let your dialogue with God unfold naturally as you honestly express any questions, doubts, or objections you feel, all the time listening for and writing down what you sense of God's responses. Continue writing until you have said all you want to say to God and feel you have "heard" all He wants to say to you. (Use another sheet of paper if you need more room.)

FURTHER EXPLORATION
of Repetition in Scripture

Exercise 1 — **Ecclesiastes 1:2-11**
A. Read Ecclesiastes 1:2-11 out loud. List all the instances of

repetition you can find in this passage (of single words, phrases, images, ideas).

B. How do these repetitions reinforce the message of this passage?

C. Do you find this passage depressing, enjoyable, or both? Why do you think you react as you do?

*Exercise 2—*2 **Timothy 2:14-26**
A. Read 2 Timothy 2:14-26. While the repetition of words and word pictures in the passages from Daniel and Ecclesiastes was quite obvious, the repetition in this passage is not immediately apparent. By listening carefully, however, for repeated words and ideas, we can discern that Paul's mind was focused principally on one particular problem Timothy was facing in his ministry. What do you think that problem was?

B. Imagine Paul had written this passage as a song. Compose a chorus (using Paul's words and your own) to sum up the main lesson Paul wanted Timothy to take away from this passage. What would you title this song of Paul's?

7

OMISSION
Drawing Us into the Story

Luke 19:1-10

INTRODUCTION

"Why didn't God make the Bible longer," my friend complained, "and fill in more details?" I could understand her frustration. Our little Bible study group was grappling with an account that raised far more questions than it answered. Was it wise of God to inspire a narrative that left so much to the imagination?

Actually, most of the stories in the Bible omit the kinds of details we expect in a novel today. They don't tell us how people look. They seldom describe the setting or time of day. They give us such brief snatches of dialogue that we assume most of the conversation must be missing. They skip parts of the action, sometimes leaving yawning gaps in the plot. They almost never spell out the character's inner thoughts or feelings. Since the biblical story-tellers consistently employed a style of empty spaces, it makes us wonder if God inspired this style for a purpose.

In fact, I believe this is the case. Omissions are God's way of allowing us to enter into these stories with imagination. When Scripture does not give us specifics, we make guesses to fill in the gaps. This isn't as difficult as it sounds. After all, Bible stories are about people, and people all through history have shared the same fundamental experiences and feelings: growing up, falling in love, raising children, worrying, playing, worshiping, laboring, gossiping, growing old. Because we are human, as the people in the Bible were human, we can guess about their actions and feelings if enough of the story is sketched in for us.

Think of the account of Noah and the ark. The story enumerates God's instructions about building the ark and loading the animals, but human interest elements are strangely lacking. Did Noah struggle with inner doubts or resentments as he was building the boat? Did his neighbors mock him? Did his wife and sons think he was crazy until the flood began?

When gaps like this mark Bible stories, it's not easy for us to relate personally to them. Preachers and writers naturally try to flesh out the accounts to make them more meaningful for us. Haven't you heard sermons about how Noah's neighbors made fun of him and how hard it was for him to obey God in the face of their scorn? These are guesses. But they are educated guesses, based on an understanding of human nature. We can feel pretty sure how Noah's neighbors reacted to his boat-building because we know how people with unpopular beliefs are ridiculed and ostracized today. We can surmise that Noah sometimes had mixed feelings as he obeyed God's instructions because we ourselves never find it easy to obey God's will when that obedience leads to rejection by others.

When we guess about the missing elements in Bible stories, our conjectures tell more about us than they do about the passage. By reading between the lines, we are inserting ourselves into the spaces in the biblical narratives. But isn't this just what God wants us to do? Once we have let our imaginations enter into the text, we are in a position where the story can touch us personally, comfort or challenge us, and make a real difference in our lives.

Two precautions are necessary. Because we recognize the authority of God's Word, we will make sure our speculations are consistent with the details the text gives us. Furthermore, we will

OMISSION

try to learn any historical or cultural background that can help us understand the stories. But if we follow these precautions, guessing to fill in the gaps is good—even if our interpretations sometimes differ. After all, if God had wanted to make sure we would all visualize a narrative in exactly the same way, He could have made the Bible longer, as my frustrated friend suggested, and filled in all the pertinent details. The fact that He did not is His invitation to us to use our imaginations. Because of His omissions, we can put ourselves into the story.

TUNING IN
to Omission

Have you sometimes felt frustrated because the Bible does not give you more details in its narratives? Name one Bible story where you wish you could have been there yourself to see what really happened. If you have your own ideas about some of the missing information in this story, write them down here.

PURSUING
Omission in Luke 19:1-10

1. Read Luke 19:1-10. The characters in this episode are Jesus, Zaccheus, and the people in the crowd. Notice that Luke, in telling the story, gives us only the information that a bystander on that day could have observed or readily surmised. Summarize below the actions of the three. Add any thoughts or feelings that Luke specifically tells us.

HOW TO HEAR THE LIVING WORD

- Jesus:

- Zaccheus:

- The Crowd:

2. Though Luke tells us little about what was going on in these people's minds and hearts that caused them to act as they did, we can make educated guesses. But understanding one bit of historical background is crucial. We need to know that tax collectors were Jews who were resented and ostracized by their fellow Jews, both because they worked for the hated Roman occupation forces and because they were notorious for cheating the people they taxed. No good Jew would eat or socialize with them; they were barred from synagogue and temple.

Trying to put yourself in Zaccheus' mind, recount the thoughts you imagine went through his head as the events of verses 1-7 unfolded. (Write this in the first person, as if you were Zaccheus.)

3. Imagine you are one of the people in the crowd and you witness Zaccheus' and Christ's actions in verses 1-7. Recount the thoughts and feelings you experience as the episode unfolds.

OMISSION

Write down comments you might have made to your friends when you heard Jesus inviting Himself to the tax collector's home.

4. After verse 7 there seems to be a gap in the plot. The scene jumps from the crowded street to the home of Zaccheus, where the tax collector announces that he will give half his possessions to the poor and pay back fourfold all those he has cheated. Based on what you know about Jesus, what do you imagine went on between Jesus and Zaccheus in this interval between verses 7 and 8?

5. In verse 10 Jesus proclaims His purpose for coming to earth: "to seek and save what was lost." In what ways can you imagine that Zaccheus was lost before he met Jesus? How did Christ's actions remedy his "lostness"?

6. The townspeople were lost too, in a different way from Zaccheus. Define their "lostness." What in Christ's actions might have served to bring them out of that lost condition?

7. At this point in your life, do you identify more with the lost condition of Zaccheus or with the lost condition of the townspeople? Explain.

8. Zaccheus climbed a tree where Jesus found him. What direction do you think you might move, what action do you think you might take, to make yourself more available to Jesus now?

9. List all the qualities of Jesus that you see as you read between the lines in this story. Which one of these qualities do you wish were more present in your own life? Why?

FURTHER EXPLORATION
of Omission in Scripture

Exercise 1 — Acts 16:16-25

A. Here is Luke's account of one dramatic confrontation Paul had with opponents in the course of his missionary travels. The incident took place in Philippi, which was a Roman colony — a city where veteran Roman soldiers settled and governed themselves. A small community of Jews lived there, and was probably viewed with suspicion by the Roman populace. The story opens with Paul and his companions headed for the Jewish place of prayer outside Philippi, a place where they had initially met and converted a woman named Lydia. Read Acts 16:16-25.

This account is typical of biblical narrative in that it has lots of conflict and action but little explicit description of what people were thinking and feeling. Imagine that you were a reporter who

OMISSION

observed the slave owners dragging Paul and Silas into the marketplace. You heard the owners' accusations and witnessed the magistrates' treatment of the missionaries, and you wanted to get to the bottom of all the commotion. What questions would you ask the following people if you had the chance to interview each of them?

- Paul:

- One of the slave owners:

- The slave girl:

- One of the magistrates:

- One of Paul's companions who had seen the exorcism:

- A Roman who had been in the marketplace crowd:

B. Choose what you think is your most intriguing question for each of the people above, and guess at the answer they would have given.

- Paul:

- The slave owner:

- The slave girl:

HOW TO HEAR THE LIVING WORD

- The magistrate:

- Paul's companion:

- A Roman in the crowd:

C. After being severely flogged, Paul and Silas were thrown into prison and confined with their feet in the stocks. Imagine the prayers they probably prayed in these circumstances and write them below.

Exercise 2 — Genesis 22:1-18

A. Read Genesis 22:1-18 aloud. Try to listen to the story as if you have never heard it before. What is your initial reaction to this narrative? Are you surprised, disgusted, terrified, inspired, what?

B. This story is highly dramatic, yet it makes no mention of emotions. How would you film the story to capture its emotional impact? What setting, lighting, sound effects, or background music would you create? What costumes would you choose for the actors, and how would you choreograph their movements? Would

OMISSION

you add more dialogue, perhaps between God and Abraham, Abraham and Isaac, or Abraham and the angel? Why or why not?

C. Though this story seems primitive and distant from our world, it demonstrates eternal truths. What are these truths? How do you feel about them?

8

HYPERBOLE
Exaggeration in the Service of Truth

Psalm 18

INTRODUCTION

"My tour of the British Isles was perfect!" a friend enthused. "They packed so much in every day, we never stopped long enough to catch our breath. We must have seen a million sights in two weeks. It cost me a fortune, but it was worth it."

Hyperbole! It's a fancy literary term for something we use every day in conversation. The dictionary defines hyperbole as "extravagant exaggeration." If we look closely at the quote above, we will see that every sentence contains phrasing that stretches, or downright strains, the bounds of truth.

When we hear hyperbolic language, we recognize instinctively that it won't bear scrutiny as factual reporting. But we also recognize that it conveys some kind of truth more effectively than a precise statement of the facts could. Our job when we meet hyperbole is to tune into the deeper truths that lie behind the literal exaggerations. Often these are truths concerning emotions or attitudes.

60

HYPERBOLE

The friend who used the extravagant words above to describe her vacation was giving a distorted view of the pace and cost of the trip, but at the same time she was conveying an accurate sense of the pleasure she herself derived from it. Her exuberant use of hyperbole gave me insight into a mind and heart still bursting with the excitement of her travels.

When we read Scripture, common sense usually tells us when to discount extreme language, reading the force of the feeling behind the words without taking them literally. For example, we hear the urgency of Jesus' call in Matthew 5:29-30 to remove the sin from our lives without feeling compelled to obey His command to pluck out the eye or cut off the hand that causes us to sin. We count on our Lord's promises concerning the power of prayer in Mark 11:23-24 without actually expecting mountains to throw themselves into the sea at our command.

It is often crucial in reading Scripture not to mistake hyperbole for literal truth. But it is also crucial not to mistake divine truth for exaggeration. Our natural skepticism tells us to automatically discount extravagant language; words like "perfect" and "forever" must be stretching the truth. But the God who reveals Himself in the Bible *is* "too good to be true," yet He is true. His nature is divine perfection and His plans do stand forever. Therefore when we read words like those in Romans that promise "there is nothing in all creation that will ever be able to separate us from the love of God which is ours through Christ Jesus our Lord" (TEV), we can put aside all skepticism and simply revel in the pure, hyperbolic truth of God's perfect love for us.

TUNING IN
to Hyperbole

What is something that you hate doing? Write two or three sentences describing that activity, using hyperbole to convey the strength of your negative feelings.

HOW TO HEAR THE LIVING WORD

PURSUING
Hyperbole in Psalm 18

1. The heading of Psalm 18 says that David sang this song to the Lord when the Lord delivered him from the hand of all his enemies. Read the psalm through, noticing all the extravagant language in it. What three words would you use to describe the psalmist's feelings, his mood as he writes these verses?

2. In verses 29-42, there are certain hyperbolic phrases describing David's prowess that suggest a comic-book hero in the "Superman" tradition. Compare these verses in two or more Bible versions. Write down the most dramatic descriptions of David's prowess that you find.

Draw some cartoon sketches (complete with appropriate words or sound effects) to reflect the pictures painted by these hyperbolic phrases.

HYPERBOLE

3. The opening words of Psalm 18, "I love You, O LORD, my strength," suggest that the central theme of this psalm is strength. In the first column below, list all the words and phrases from verses 1-3 and 29-42 that suggest God's strength. In the second column, list all the words and phrases that suggest David's strength and prowess.

God's strength	*David's strength*

4. Comparing these two columns of words and phrases, how is David's strength different from God's strength? What is the relationship of David's strength and God's strength?

5. God can give many kinds of strength. Psalm 18 speaks of Him giving David physical strength and preeminence in battle. What other kinds of strength do you think God gives?

What kinds of strength have you experienced God giving you? Explain.

6. You may feel the need for God's strength right now because you are in some kind of battle—perhaps a battle with illness, or with another person's antagonism, or with the pressure of difficult circumstances, or with a bad habit or attitude. Read Psalm 18 again. What phrases in it particularly speak to you in the midst of your current battle? Why?

7. Imagine that God has already brought you victory in this battle. Write a psalm of triumph and thanksgiving similar to David's. Fill it with concrete pictures of God's strength and with specific descriptions of the ways He has strengthened you and brought you through your battle. (Use a separate sheet of paper if you need more room.)

HYPERBOLE

FURTHER EXPLORATION
of Hyperbole in Scripture

Exercise 1 — 1 Corinthians 13:1-3
A. Paul wrote these familiar verses to the Corinthian Christians who had apparently developed a proud, competitive attitude concerning the spiritual gifts God had given them — gifts like speaking in tongues, prophecy, faith, and giving. What exaggerated phrases does Paul use to mimic and mock the pride the Corinthians feel about each of these gifts?

B. Think of the various gifts people in your own church display, gifts which may lead them into pride and competitiveness. Write a modern version of Paul's warnings in 1 Corinthians 13. You might begin, "If I sing solos with the virtuosity of a mockingbird, but have not love, I am only a barking dog or a squeaky hinge."

C. Try to pinpoint the one gift you have that is most likely to lead you into pride. Write a hyperbolic warning aimed at yourself, following Paul's pattern ("If I . . . but have not love, I am . . ."). If pride in this area is something you struggle with often, you may want to make a poster or plaque of this warning and place it where it will be a helpful reminder to you.

HOW TO HEAR THE LIVING WORD

Exercise 2—**Micah 7:2-4a**

A. Are you an emotional, hyperbolic kind of person? Or do you tend to be cautious and restrained? Put a mark on the scale below to indicate how you see yourself.

Hyperbolic *Restrained*

|—————+—————+—————+—————+—————+—————+—————+—————|

B. Read Micah 7:2-4a. Here is the Prophet Micah's description of the ungodly society he lives in. His hyperbolic language expresses his own feelings, and because he is a prophet, it also expresses God's assessment of the situation.

If you heard someone saying these same things about our current society, how would you react? What thoughts and feelings would the denunciation call up in you?

How much do you think your reaction has to do with your personality type, as indicated in Question A?

C. What is the value of seeing things in exaggerated, black-and-white terms, as Micah does in this passage?

What are the dangers of seeing things in such all-or-nothing ways?

9

POETIC JUSTICE
The Good Guys Win; The Bad Guys Lose

Revelation 17:1-6; 18:1–19:9

INTRODUCTION

Remember *Star Wars,* the intergalactic adventure movie which pitted noble rebel troops against the evil forces of the Empire? The Empire planned to squelch the rebellion with its ultimate weapon, the Death Star, which could instantly blow up a whole planet. But just as the rebel base was about to be destroyed, Luke Skywalker dropped a bomb that blew the Death Star to smithereens. As this evil instrument of terror disappeared in a burst of smoke and fire that filled the screen, the audience cheered.

Here was a perfect example of poetic justice, and of how we respond to such justice. At the climax of countless dramas we have felt this same upsurge of satisfaction when the bad guys are defeated and the good guys triumph. It seems that built into each of us is a deep desire for things to turn out right. We want reassurance that people get what they deserve, that justice operates at the heart of the universe.

HOW TO HEAR THE LIVING WORD

The Bible teaches us that the God who reigns over the universe is just. In its pages we find frequent examples of His justice, with the godly emerging triumphant and the wicked paying the price for their sins. But the Bible also acknowledges that in this world godly people often suffer while the wicked and selfish prosper.

God knows that we struggle with the apparent unfairness of much of life. I think that is why He sprinkles so many instances of poetic justice throughout His Word. There's a tidiness that's reassuring in the way poetic justice operates. The good guys always get rescued before it's too late and the bad guys always get punished in perfectly appropriate ways. When we meet these neat examples of justice, they help us believe what is ultimately true: God's perfect justice will someday triumph over the forces of evil and injustice that seem to hold sway in our world.

Naturally, we will feel cheered when we see the good guys rewarded in Scripture. Naturally, we will cheer when we see the bad guys punished. Yet even as we cheer, there ought to be a catch in our voices. Our satisfaction when the good guys win and the bad guys lose can never be self-satisfaction. We too are sinners. From the standpoint of pure justice, we deserve destruction along with all the bad guys. Only because God in His mercy sent His Son to pay the price for our sins and be our righteousness can we number ourselves among the good guys.

In some sense we should weep, not cheer, when we read of God punishing the wicked. After all, in the Old Testament we often see God himself agonizing over the punishment He has to bring on ungodly people. Peter assures us in his epistle that the Lord does not want anyone to perish, but He wants "everyone to come to repentance" (2 Peter 3:9).

Nevertheless, judgment must come and those who ignore or defy God must be destroyed. God's ultimate goal is to establish a kingdom of perfect peace, joy, and righteousness, and He will not allow evil to spoil His plans. Because we belong to God, we feel a keen sense of satisfaction, a legitimate pleasure, and a profound hope whenever we read in the Bible of godly people succeeding while the wicked fall. Each picture of poetic justice is like a little piece of God's ultimate triumph which He gives us to savor now as a foretaste of the final perfect justice He will bring.

POETIC JUSTICE

TUNING IN
to Poetic Justice

Think of a favorite story of yours (novel, film, TV show, fairy tale, etc.) where the good guys triumph in the end and the bad guys get what they deserve. Briefly summarize the climax of the story.

PURSUING
Poetic Justice in Revelation 17, 18, and 19

1. In the closing chapters of Revelation, John has a vision of the last days when God's final judgment will come and the new heaven and the new earth will be established. In chapters 17 and 18 and the beginning of chapter 19, the focus is on the fall of Babylon, a city portrayed as a great prostitute. This city represents the ultimate in worldly decadence, a kingdom where selfishness, materialism, and idolatry reign and godly people are persecuted. Read Revelation 17:1-6, 18:1-24, and 19:1-9. Note in the margins the spontaneous emotions you feel as you read through this passage.

2. List all the sins of Babylon that are mentioned or implied in 17:1-6 and 18:1-24.

Why do you think "adultery" and "prostitution" are appropriate metaphors to sum up the essential wickedness of Babylon?

3. Babylon, before her destruction, illustrated perfectly the blatant unfairness we often meet in this world. This city was fabulously prosperous, popular, and powerful, even though she flouted God's Law. Meanwhile, godly people who lived in her were suffering and dying. Name one situation in our current world where similar unfairness exists, with the wicked succeeding while the good suffer.

- How does seeing this unfairness make you feel?

- How do you think God wants you to feel about it?

- What do you wish God would do about this unfair situation?

4. Read the following passages about Babylon's downfall. How does each portray punishments that seem perfectly suited to Babylon's sins?

Revelation 18:2, 21-23

POETIC JUSTICE

Revelation 18:5-8

5. Poetic justice is often expressed in a reversal of fortunes, with the proud being humbled while the humble are exalted. The salvation Jesus brought was repeatedly described in terms of radical reversal: "The last will be first, and the first will be last" (Matthew 20:16). The hungry will be "filled ... with good things" but the rich will be "sent away empty" (Luke 1:53).

John's vision paints just such a reversal, with sharp contrasts between 18:1-24 and 19:1-9. Choose one of the following ways to make this reversal more vivid for yourself:

a. Read Revelation 18:1–19:9 aloud dramatically, using appropriate tones of voice for the various speakers.

b. Make a collage that represents the downfall of Babylon contrasted with the exaltation of God's saints.

c. Drawing on all the assigned passages from Revelation 17:1 to Revelation 19:9, pick out key phrases that capture the progression from Babylon's glory to her destruction. Then pick out key phrases that capture the progression from the saints' suffering to their triumph. Write these phrases below. Then make a poster with these two sets of phrases arranged and written in such a way that their meaning and impact will be emphasized.

6. Are you now personally involved in a situation where life seems unfair? Describe the feelings you have struggled with in this situation.

How do the passages you have just read in Revelation 17–19 help you cope with that unfairness and with your feelings? (If there are two or three verses in the passages that you find particularly encouraging, you may want to memorize them.)

FURTHER EXPLORATION
of Poetic Justice in Scripture

Exercise 1 — **Matthew 18:23-35**
A. Read the Parable of the Unmerciful Servant in Matthew 18:23-35. Summarize what happens in the three acts of this dramatic little story.

ACT I:

ACT II:

POETIC JUSTICE

ACT III:

B. Why is this parable a good example of poetic justice? How do you feel about how the master treats the first servant at the end of the story?

C. In one sentence of 10 words or less, state the lesson you think Jesus wants to teach us through this parable. (For help, read verses 21-22 that lead into the parable.)

D. Is there someone you are failing to forgive right now? How do you react to the thought that God will treat you as the master treated the first servant at the end?

Exercise 2 — Genesis 25:24-28; 27:1-35; 37:1-35
A. Sometimes the Bible pictures God actively visiting appropriate punishments on sinners. At other times, poetic justice seems to operate more subtly as people suffer the logical consequences for their choices and actions. Hosea speaks of how those who "sow the wind" will "reap the whirlwind."

HOW TO HEAR THE LIVING WORD

Read Genesis 25:24-28 and 27:1-35, accounts about Jacob's early life. Then read Genesis 37:1-35, an account from much later in Jacob's life. In what ways do you see poetic justice operating in Jacob's life?

B. Recall a time in your life when your own wrong choices or behavior came back to haunt you, when you in a sense "fell into a pit that you yourself had dug"? Briefly recount what happened.

C. Do you think it is more helpful for you to view that incident from your life as an instance of God personally punishing you for your sin, or as an example of an impersonal natural law of cause and effect working itself out in your life? Explain.

Which explanation do you think is closer to the truth? Why?

10

PARADOX
Beyond the Limits of Logic

Ephesians 1:3-23; 5:1-20

INTRODUCTION

Can believers ever lose their salvation? Some would say "No, never!" For support they would point to Jesus' words in John 10:27-29,

> My sheep listen to My voice; I know them, and they follow Me. I give them eternal life and they shall never perish; no one can snatch them out of My hand. My Father, who has given them to Me, is greater than all; no one can snatch them out of My Father's hand.

Others, however, would contend that those who have accepted Christ can forfeit their salvation by later turning their backs on Him. That is the apparent meaning of Jesus' words in John 15:1-2, 6.

> I am the true vine and My Father is the gardener. He cuts off every branch in Me that bears no fruit.... If anyone does

not remain in Me, he is like a branch that is thrown away and withers; such branches are picked up, thrown into the fire and burned.

What we have here is a paradox. Two biblical pictures apparently contradict each other, yet we know both must be true since both are found in the authoritative Word of God.

Sometimes the contradictions in Scripture appear in different passages or different books; sometimes they are squeezed into the space of a few words, as when Paul says, "For when I am weak, then I am strong" (2 Corinthians 12:10). Rarely are biblical paradoxes simply catchy wording used to dress up straightforward truths. Rather, they embody the profound mysteries of our faith. Over the centuries theologians have struggled to wrestle these paradoxes into clear doctrinal positions, but their "solutions" consistently contradict each other. Thus their efforts underline the fact that most of the paradoxes in the Bible lie beyond the scope of rational resolution.

Below are just some of the unanswerable questions the Bible raises.

- How can God's nature combine perfect justice and infinite mercy?
- In a universe under God's sovereign rule, how can human beings exercise free will?
- How can Jesus Christ be fully God and fully man?
- How can we be new creatures in Christ while the old nature still operates in us?
- How can Christians be *in* this world but not *of* it?

What do we do with these paradoxes in Scripture? I think most of us feel compelled to struggle with them intellectually, searching for satisfactory answers. In the case of the question about whether or not Christians can lose their salvation, we discover there are different doctrinal traditions to choose from. Calvinists put a greater emphasis on God's sovereign rule (and therefore predestination) and insist that God's chosen have eternal security. Arminians see free will playing a larger part in salvation, and believe people

PARADOX

can fall away from the faith and forfeit their salvation.

There is value, of course, in engaging in theological study and discussion to try to pin down what the Bible teaches. But there is also value in acknowledging that many tensions in Scripture will not be tamed by the human mind. Often these tensions express themselves in stories or word pictures that resist intellectual analysis. Instead they invite us to experience contradictions imaginatively, learning to say yes to both sides of the truth.

Responding to the comforting picture of Jesus as shepherd in John 10:27-29, we can say, "Yes, Lord, I rest in Your assurance that You will never let me go." Responding to the rather chilling picture of God the gardener in John 15:1-2 and 6, we must say, "Yes, Lord, I hear Your warning about what will happen if I fail to hold on to You." As we enter into these paradoxical portrayals of security and danger, our commitment to our Lord will be strengthened and stretched.

Biblical paradoxes serve to stimulate our minds to wrestle with truth. But in the end they bring us to the limits of logic. The contradictions in God's Word, unreconciled and unreconcilable, force us to our knees before the mystery of life. They remind us that only by faith can we make our way through the complexities of a world saturated by sin and permeated by God's grace.

TUNING IN
to Paradox

Can you add to the list of biblical paradoxes given in the introduction? What paradox in Scripture do you find the most frustrating, and why?

PURSUING
Paradox in Ephesians 1:3-23; 5:1-20

1. How do we come to know Christ and grow more like Him? Is sanctification something God accomplishes in us, or something we achieve to please Him? Should we work hard at becoming better Christians, or should we relax and trust Him to do His perfecting work in us?

This whole question of sanctification is an area of tension in the New Testament. The paradox is captured in this verse from Philippians:

> Therefore, my dear friends, as you have always obeyed—not only in my presence, but now much more in my absence—continue to work out your salvation with fear and trembling, for it is God who works in you to will and to act according to His good purpose (Philippians 2:12-13).

Read Ephesians 1:3-23. Make a list of all the verbs and verb phrases that describe what God does for believers. Then list all the verbs that describe the believer's role. (Notice how many of the verbs in the second column are passive.)

God's Role	Believer's Role
Example: "blessed us" (v. 3)	"to be adopted" (v. 5)

2. Read Ephesians 5:1-20. List all the things that Paul commands believers to do. Then list all the things that Paul says God through Christ does for believers.

PARADOX

Responsibility of Believers	**God's Work**
Example: be imitators of God (v. 1)	love us (vv. 1-2)

3. Based on these two sets of lists, how would you describe the balance (or tension) between what God contributes and what believers contribute to the process of growing in the faith?

4. What do we gain from focusing on *God's role* in our growth? What drawbacks might there be in emphasizing this side of the paradox of sanctification?

HOW TO HEAR THE LIVING WORD

5. What do we gain from focusing on *our role* in our growth? What drawbacks might there be in emphasizing this side of the paradox of sanctification?

6. Based on the Christians you know, do you think the church today needs to put a greater emphasis on trusting God for spiritual growth, or on the importance of discipline and effort in the Christian life? Defend your position.

7. Among the phrases you found in Ephesians 1:3-23 (see Question 1), what is one phrase you really need to hear right now? Why?

8. Among the phrases you found in Ephesians 5:1-20 (see Question 2), what is one phrase you really need to hear right now? Why?

FURTHER EXPLORATION
of Paradox in Scripture

Exercise 1—**Paradoxes surrounding prayer**
A. Read the two sets of verses below: What paradox do you find in

these verses concerning how we should pray and what answers we should expect?

Matthew 6:9-10 **Mark 14:32-36**	**Matthew 21:18-22** **John 15:7**

B. Think of something you want very badly, and write a prayer based on the model suggested by the first set of verses. Then rewrite the prayer based on Jesus' teaching in the second set of verses.

C. Which of the two prayers above is more like the prayers you have been praying? Will you pray differently after reading these verses? Why or why not?

Exercise 2— **Paradoxes surrounding women's roles**
A. Read Genesis 1:27-28 and Genesis 2:20-24. What tension do you sense between the role of women described in Genesis 1 and the role described in Genesis 2?

B. Read 1 Corinthians 11:3-12. How does Paul in these verses struggle with the same tension that was evident in the Creation passages?

C. The God-ordained role of women is the subject of much debate among Christians at present. Does focusing on the tensions in the passages above cause you to rethink your position in this debate? Explain.

11

DRAMATIC IRONY
We Know Something They Don't Know

Luke 24:1-35

INTRODUCTION

Recently I was invited to a surprise birthday party for a close friend. It was exciting being in on plans that Beth knew nothing about. I could see how her words and actions were particularly appropriate or inappropriate in light of the celebration that was coming, yet she remained unaware of their significance. One day, for example, she confided to me, "My husband and I are going to have a nice quiet dinner at Giorgio's to celebrate my birthday." I could barely contain my amusement, thinking of all the friends and relatives who would joyfully shout "Surprise!" when she arrived for her "nice quiet" celebration.

Why is it so much fun to be invited to a surprise party? Because there's a gratifying sense of being in the inner circle, privy to knowledge even the birthday person does not possess. There's pleasurable suspense in wondering if and when the person will catch on to the secret. And there's satisfaction in watching the reaction when the person finally puts all the puzzle pieces together and figures out how the plan developed without his or her knowledge.

Dramatic irony in a story puts the reader in a position similar to that of someone invited to a surprise party. The author lets us know crucial information that a character or characters in the story are unaware of. Armed with this special knowledge, we listen to their words and view their actions with heightened interest. We're delighted to catch them doing or saying things that have a special humor or poignancy that they aren't aware of.

Biblical narratives often incorporate dramatic irony. Perhaps this is because God has done so many surprising things throughout history, and the Bible allows us to watch these surprises develop, though the people who are experiencing them at the time cannot see what God is doing.

Of course, God's most magnificent surprise was sending His own Son to save us by dying for us. When we read the Gospels, we know who Jesus was and why He came, but the people who interact with Jesus in the stories frequently misunderstand His person and purpose. This often produces powerful dramatic irony. A good example is found in accounts of the way the Roman soldiers treated Jesus before He died. Jesus had told Pilate that He was the King of the Jews, but the soldiers understood nothing of God's exalted plans for His Son. When they put a purple robe around His shoulders and a crown of thorns on His head and fell down on their knees to worship Him, their actions were intended as savage mockery. Reading of their behavior, we are in one sense pained and appalled to witness our Lord subjected to such cruelty. But in another sense we feel profound awe and satisfaction because we see that God was in control of this whole drama. The soldiers were unwittingly acknowledging Jesus' true majesty even as they mocked Him. Later when they crucified Him, they thought they were carrying out the wishes of the Jewish leaders and the Roman authorities, but in actuality they were carrying out the very purposes of God Himself.

Dramatic irony like this in Scripture gives us far more pleasure than such irony can provide in any other literature. For in the Bible we are not simply allowed to share the knowledge of a human author about His characters and their fate. Rather, God

DRAMATIC IRONY

Himself as Author of history shares with us the special surprises He holds in store for individuals and for all humanity. How exciting to be invited into God's confidence in this way. How privileged we are, as believers and Bible readers, to be in on the best surprise party ever.

TUNING IN
to Dramatic Irony

Recall a time when you were involved in a surprise for another person. Did that person say or do anything that was funny or ironic in light of the surprise that awaited? What? How did it make you feel being in on the scheme while he or she was unaware of the plans?

PURSUING
Dramatic Irony in Luke 24:1-35

1. Read Luke 24:1-12. These verses tell about the first Easter morning, when Jesus' followers were confronted with the surprising truth that their Lord had risen from the tomb. Try to imagine how you would have felt if you had been there. Why do you think the women (vv. 1-8) were able to believe the good news? Why do you think the men (vv. 9-11) did not believe?

2. Later that same day, two of the men were walking to Emmaus, a village near Jerusalem, when Jesus joined them. Read Luke

HOW TO HEAR THE LIVING WORD

24:13-35. Dramatic irony contributes much to this account. Where does the irony come out most strongly?

What does dramatic irony add to this story for you? Does it make it more amusing? More suspenseful? More inspiring? Explain.

3. How does the failure of the two men to recognize the risen Lord and believe in Him make you feel about them?

4. What feelings do you think Jesus had toward these two as He walked along talking with them? Why?

5. Why do you think Christ kept His identity hidden from them for so long? In your mind rewrite the story with Jesus clearly identifying Himself as soon as He joins the men on the road. What might the men have missed if He had chosen to do this?

DRAMATIC IRONY

6. In this account, starting with v. 11, the two men go through various stages as they journey from disbelief to belief. Outline these stages here.

7. Which of these stages mirrors your own spiritual journey in coming to believe that Jesus Christ is your living Lord? Explain.

8. If we accept the biblical accounts about Jesus rising from the tomb, we have assurance that He is alive now and always present with us. Yet there are times for each of us when we do not recognize Him walking along beside us. Perhaps we yearn to have Him close but cannot feel His presence during difficult circumstances. Or perhaps we choose to ignore Him for a time while we go our own way. Only later are we surprised to see that He was with us all the time and was accomplishing His purposes in and through us.

Write a brief account of a time like this in your own life. What kept you from feeling Christ's presence and power during that time? Later, what did you discover He had accomplished while you thought He was absent?

HOW TO HEAR THE LIVING WORD

FURTHER EXPLORATION
of Dramatic Irony in Scripture

Exercise 1a — **2 Samuel 11:1-27**
A. Read through 2 Samuel 11:1-27, which tells the story of David's sin with Bathsheba and how he tries to cover up that sin. The principal actors in this drama are David, Uriah, and Joab. Devise a chart which will show a comparison of these three personalities based on the behavior they display in this passage. You may need to use a separate sheet of paper for this exercise.

B. Uriah is really the hero of this story, the "good guy," yet he is the ignorant one. We as readers see him unwittingly saying and doing things that seal his own doom. What are these things?

DRAMATIC IRONY

C. Reread verse 11. Explain the dramatic irony in these words, their special significance that we as readers recognize in light of verses 1-4, but that Uriah himself does not recognize.

Do you think David recognized at this time the relevance of Uriah's words to his own actions? Why or why not?

D. What feelings do you have toward Uriah when you see him unwittingly making choices that will lead to tragic consequences?

E. What feelings toward David come to you when you see Uriah as the innocent victim of David's schemes?

Exercise 1b — 2 Samuel 12:1-13

A. In these verses, the consequences of David's sin with Bathsheba continue to be played out. Read 2 Samuel 12:1-13. Who is the "schemer" who is privy to secret knowledge in this passage? Who has the role of the "ignorant one," the victim of the scheme?

B. As you read the parable Nathan tells (vv. 1-4), do you immediately see the parallels to the sins David has committed? What are those parallels?

C. Verses 5-7a are the pivotal point in the dramatic irony that operates in this passage. How do you react to these verses?

D. Compare your reaction to the dramatic irony in 2 Samuel 12 where David is the victim and Nathan the schemer to your reaction in the previous chapter where Uriah is the victim and David the schemer. What makes the difference?

12

ECHOES
Connecting Past, Present, and Future

Selected Old and New Testament Passages

INTRODUCTION

As we get to know people, consistent life-patterns become apparent to us. We notice their pet peeves, the TV programs they prefer, how they deal with deadlines, who they invite to parties. After we've witnessed the same kinds of choices and reactions over and over, their behavior becomes more or less predictable. We realize that the present shape of their lives mirrors their past, and that their past give us a window into their future.

As we read the Bible we are getting to know God, and the more we read, the more we notice consistent patterns emerging in His Word. God relates to sinful humans in similar ways in Old and New Testaments. Early events in the Bible often foreshadow later ones, and later texts allude to what earlier authors have said. Dramatic plot elements and word pictures appear over and over again.

That such echoes abound in Scripture may surprise us when we remember that many different authors wrote the various books of the Bible in different places and over a long span of time. But the repetitions are testimony to the fact that there was really only one Author behind the Bible—one God creating one great story of salvation.

All kinds of themes, patterns, and pictures echo through Scripture, but as we would expect, it is the saving events that echo loudest. The preeminent redemptive event of Old Testament history was the Exodus, when God brought His people out of slavery and into the Promised Land. Allusions to this event appear over and over in the Old Testament. Isaiah, for example, in his prophecies of how God will lead the exiles out of captivity in Babylon, gives us pictures reminiscent of the parting of the Red Sea and the miraculous provision of water in the wilderness.

> When you pass through the waters, I will be with you; and when you pass through the rivers, they will not sweep over you. . . . I provide water in the desert and streams in the wasteland, to give drink to My people, My chosen (Isaiah 43:2, 20).

There are echoes of the Exodus too in the life of Jesus. In miraculously feeding the 5,000 and then calling Himself the Bread from heaven, Jesus purposely identified Himself with the manna that God sent the Israelites in the wilderness. In dying on the cross at Passover time, He both reenacted and amplified the sacrifice of the lambs whose blood protected God's people from death and set them free from bondage during the first Passover.

Tuning in to the repeated themes and motifs in Scripture is like hearing the harmonies of a song weave themselves together. We gain a much deeper sense of the beauty and meaning in God's Word. We also become convinced that the One who authored the story of the Bible always remains true to His nature, and can be counted on to continue writing that story until all His perfect plans have been fulfilled. In fact, we find He has written us into the story. The patterns that appear in the Old and New Testaments, patterns of human failure and divine righteousness and grace, are part of our own daily experience. Consequently, as we listen for

ECHOES

the echoes in God's Word, we hear responsive echoes in our own hearts. God has drawn us into His great drama of salvation.

TUNING IN
to Echoes

As people come to know you well, what is one pattern you think they see repeated in your speech or actions that gives them a crucial clue to the essential shape of your personality and priorities?

PURSUING
Echoes of the Marriage between God and His People

1. The Old Testament prophets repeatedly pictured God as the husband of the nation of Israel. The marriage images they used told the story of a rocky relationship that rivals the most melodramatic of soap operas. While various prophets show us different scenes from the marriage, if we put the scenes together in our minds, we find ourselves caught up in a great drama of love and betrayal, jealousy and anger, forgiveness and reconciliation.

Sample the way the prophets portray the marriage between God and Israel by reading Ezekiel 16:1-22, 35-42 and Isaiah 54:4-8; 62:2-5. (You may also want to read Hosea 2:2-23 and Jeremiah 2:1-5; 3:6-15.) Based on these passages, how would you describe the main acts in the Old Testament drama of God's marriage with His chosen people?

ACT I

ACT II

ACT III

ACT IV

2. Have you experienced echoes of this Old Testament marriage drama in your own relationship with God? Explain.

3. In the New Testament we can hear echoes of the divine/human marriage theme when Jesus is referred to as a bridegroom. Read Luke 5:33-35 and John 3:22-30. Where do you think Jesus fits into the marriage drama you outlined in your answer to Question 1? Is He part of one or more of the acts you outlined, or is His appearance a whole new act in the drama? Explain.

4. While Jesus is pictured as a bridegroom in the Gospel passages, His bride is hardly mentioned. But elsewhere in the New Testament we see the bride portrayed. Read 2 Corinthians 11:2; Ephesians 5:25-27; Revelation 19:6-9; 21:2. What picture of the bride do you gain from these passages? Who is she? What is she like?

What is the relationship like between Jesus and His bride?

ECHOES

5. Even if you are a man, try to picture yourself as the bride of Christ. What can you expect of Christ as your husband? What kind of "wife" do you want to be to Him? (Try answering this question by writing out the vows you and Jesus would exchange in a wedding ceremony.)

FURTHER EXPLORATION
of Echoes in Scripture

Exercise 1 — **Echoes of drinking the cup God gives**

A. Read Matthew 26:36-46 and John 18:3-11. Jesus is contemplating His impending crucifixion, but He refers to it as a cup that He must drink. Why do you think Jesus uses this strange picture for His death? How does the picture affect you?

B. Now read these Old Testament passages which echo the image of a cup that God gives people to drink: Psalm 75; Jeremiah 25:15-17, 27-29; Habakkuk 2:16-17. As this image threads its way through the Old Testament, what meaning does it have? What is the cup full of, and why does God make people drink it?

C. Does knowing the Old Testament background of the "cup" image Jesus used before His crucifixion help you understand the true meaning of His death? Explain.

D. The next time you drink from the cup during the sacrament of the Lord's Supper, try remembering the image Jesus used of drinking from the cup His Father gave Him. How do you think this might deepen the meaning of communion for you?

Exercise 2—Echoes of God's preference in choosing people to serve Him

A. When God chooses people to be part of His redemptive plan, a pattern of preference emerges that goes counter to the way the world usually chooses. Read the following Old Testament passages: Genesis 25:21-26; 27:34-37; 37:5-10; 45:1-11; Deuteronomy 7:6-8; 1 Samuel 16:1-13. What common threads run through God's choices here?

B. How do you see echoes of the same pattern in each of the following New Testament passages?

Mark 2:13-19

Mark 10:13-16

ECHOES

Luke 2:8-12

Luke 22:24-27

1 Corinthians 1:22-25

Philippians 2:5-9

C. As a believer, you have been chosen by God to be part of the redemptive plan that He set in motion in the Bible. Write a verse about yourself being chosen by God that echoes the pattern that you saw in the Old and New Testament verses above.

WRAP-UP
Putting What You've Learned to Work

This book has taught you to recognize twelve literary elements frequently found in the Bible. You've practiced a wide variety of strategies that can help you get into a passage and participate in its meaning and its power. You've discovered that literary approaches work with all kinds of biblical literature. You now have the tools to pursue literary paths into almost any Bible passage you want to study or teach. The purpose of this closing section is to demonstrate four steps you can follow to determine which paths will work best when you are preparing to lead a group in studying a particular passage.

To illustrate these steps, focus on this passage from James. As you read the passage, note the many literary elements it includes.

> We all stumble in many ways. If anyone is never at fault in what he says, he is a perfect man, able to keep his whole body in check.

When we put bits into the mouths of horses to make them obey us, we can turn the whole animal. Or take ships as an example. Although they are so large and are driven by strong winds, they are steered by a very small rudder wherever the pilot wants to go. Likewise the tongue is a small part of the body, but it makes great boasts. Consider what a great forest is set on fire by a small spark. The tongue is also a fire, a world of evil among the parts of the body. It corrupts the whole person, sets the whole course of his life on fire, and is itself set on fire by hell.

All kinds of animals, birds, reptiles, and creatures of the sea are being tamed and have been tamed by man, but no man can tame the tongue. It is a restless evil, full of deadly poison.

With the tongue we praise our Lord and Father, and with it we curse men, who have been made in God's likeness. Out of the same mouth come praise and cursing. My brothers, this should not be. Can both fresh water and salt water flow from the same spring? My brothers, can a fig tree bear olives, or a grapevine bear figs? Neither can a salt spring produce fresh water.

—James 3:2-12

STEP 1
Identify the Literary Elements in the Passage

Read a passage through at least three times, asking yourself if you see any literary elements operating. Some elements will be obvious on the first reading, while others will be harder to spot. Here are the literary elements I find in James 3:2-12, beginning with those which are most obvious.

- **Imagery**—The passage opens with the picture of stumbling which can appeal both to sight and to the internal sensation of losing one's balance, and closes with imagery of salt water and fresh water that appeals to the sense of taste. In between are numerous images that appeal to all our senses.

- **Analogy**—The tongue is compared to a horse's bit, a ship's rudder, a spark that starts a forest fire, and a poisonous snake. The mouth is compared to a spring.

- **Repetition**—In the analogies we see repeated themes: big things are guided by small things; sources like springs or fruit trees should provide the appropriate product. Words are also repeated for emphasis, as in these two verses: "The *tongue* is a *small part of the body,* but it makes *great* boasts. Consider what a *great* forest is *set on fire* by a *small* spark. The *tongue* is also a *fire,* a world of evil among the *parts of the body.* It corrupts the *whole* person, *sets* the *whole* course of his life *on fire,* and is itself *set on fire* by hell."

- **Contrast and Paradox**—James uses contrasts to point up paradoxical truths. The words *whole, large,* and *great* set over against the word *small* emphasize the apparent contradiction of small things (bit, rudder, spark, tongue) being able to control much bigger things (a horse, ship, forest fire, or a person's whole life). Then James points out the puzzling truth that people who have the ability to tame all kinds of wild animals cannot tame the tongue, a very small part of their own body. The sense of paradox deepens when James says, "With the tongue we praise our Lord and Father, and with it we curse men, who have been made in God's likeness.... This should not be. Can both fresh water and salt water flow from the same spring?" Here we have the tension of goodness and evil operating in people at the same time.

- **Conflict**—Internal struggle is suggested in the first paragraph: people are at odds with their own bodies, their own natural impulses, which will cause them to stumble if not kept in check. Internal conflict also appears in the last paragraph where praise and cursing are seen to come out of the same person.

- **Tone**—The wording in this passage suggests changing tones of voice. James begins with a reasoned, cautionary tone as he explains why we must keep our tongues in check. But we can imagine the tone becoming angrier as James speaks about the corrupting, poisonous power of the tongue. In the last paragraph we may

WRAP-UP

hear a pleading tone as James addresses his brothers in Christ.

• **Hyperbole**—James starts out mildly, suggesting that everyone will be at fault sometimes in what he says. But by verse 6 he is using hyperbole to emphasize the dangers of the tongue, implying that nothing good can ever come out of our mouths. The tongue is "a world of evil among the parts of the body. It corrupts the whole person, sets the whole course of his life on fire, and is itself set on fire by hell. . . . It is a restless evil, full of deadly poison."

• **Echoes**—In James' reference to humans taming all kinds of animals but not being able to tame the tongue which is full of deadly poison, we hear echoes of the creation account where Adam and Eve were given authority to subdue the animals, yet fell under the power of the serpent who poisoned their minds and brought death into their world.

STEP 2
Decide What Element(s) to Focus On

In developing a group study of a rich passage like James 3:2-12, you'll want to focus people's attention on one or two (at most, three) literary elements. If you are uncertain which literary paths to pursue in your group, try to approach the passage from different angles as you do your own individual study. The paths that take you deepest into the text will be good ones to use with your group. You also may want, however, to include among the elements you focus on one which was not particularly productive for you. Remember that some people in your group probably respond to different avenues of learning than you do.

In James 3:2-12, analogies carried by concrete images clearly point us most quickly to James' central concern—the dangers of the tongue. Repetition and contrast basically serve to heighten the force of these analogies and images. The other literary elements provide less direct access to the heart of the passage, though they might yield interesting insight in a group. For purposes of this demonstration, we will choose to focus on analogy and imagery as we proceed to develop a study of James 3:2-12.

STEP 3
Consider Learning Strategies Suitable for Your Focus

Once you have chosen the literary elements to pursue in a passage, you'll need to decide on strategies that will effectively involve people in those elements. At the end of the book is a checklist that summarizes the strategies employed in the preceding sessions with page numbers so you can refresh your memory on how each strategy worked for specific passages. Take a moment to turn there now and glance at the array of resources available to you.

Most strategies can be applied to several different literary elements, not just one. For example, many of the strategies on the list could work well with the analogies in the James passage. Here are just some of the possibilities:

- Have people explore the force of each analogy, listing all the ways they can think of that the tongue is like a bit, rudder, spark, poisonous snake, or spring.
- Invite people to participate fully in each image. For example, what different sensations and emotions does the image of a forest fire evoke in them? How does this make the dangers of the tongue more real to them?
- Encourage people to draw pictures suggested by the images.
- Direct people to write their own metaphors for the tongue, perhaps using images more in tune with our technological society than those of horses, ships, snakes, or springs of water.
- Ask people to recall a time when another's words, or their own, played the role of rudder, spark, snake, or spring.
- Assign groups to write and perform skits that illustrate the lessons taught by the different analogies (For example, plan a skit showing how both fresh- and saltwater words can come out of the same mouth).
- Invite people to write song lyrics around one of the startling analogies. (Example: "Your tongue started a fire and I've been burned. One vicious lie destroyed my life—there's nowhere left to turn.")
- Ask people, "Which image/metaphor hits you hardest? Why?"

WRAP-UP

STEP 4
Choose the Strategies You Want to Use

All the strategies above could be effective in a small group. In choosing the ones you want to use, keep these factors in mind.

- Your time in a group is limited. Confining your study to a few carefully chosen questions or activities will allow people time enough to thoroughly explore their own responses and to share thoughts and feelings with one another.
- Approaches don't have to be "heavy" to be effective. People may learn as much from writing a skit as from writing a prayer.
- Personalities and tastes differ. If you find that people in your group resist certain kinds of activities, choose other approaches that will seem more challenging or less threatening to them.
- Different strategies may teach the same lessons or accomplish the same purposes. Avoid asking your group to go over the same ground repeatedly. Instead, choose exercises that flow in a natural progression, moving people to get fully involved in the passage in order to experience its truths more personally.

As you experiment with literary approaches, you will discover what a powerful tool they can be in Bible study. Consider how far the four sample questions below, all built around the analogies in James 3:2-12, could take a group.

1. Meditate on James' analogies, then discuss all the ways the tongue may be like ...

a bit
a rudder
a spark
a snake
a spring

2. Think of a person whose words had either a positive or a negative effect on you during the past week. Which of James' metaphors (bit, rudder, spark, snake, or spring) would you use to describe that person's tongue? Why?

3. Think of your own mouth as a spring. Recall and write down some "freshwater" words that flowed from you this past week. Then write down some words you spoke that were "saltwater" to someone.

4. Call up in your imagination pictures of a spring of clear, pure water. Would you like such "fresh water" to flow more consistently from your own mouth? What do you think needs to change within you to make this happen?

Questions like these based on literary elements plunge us into a passage very quickly. Because they involve every part of our beings, they force *observation, interpretation,* and *application* all at once. Furthermore, as people in a group use these approaches to participate more fully in Scripture, they will also share more deeply in one another's lives.

This book has shown you the power and excitement that flow out of literary approaches to Scripture. You can purposely plug into that power and experience that excitement. The checklist that follows summarizes the strategies used in this book to mine the literary richness of the Bible. Take these strategies, mix and match them, add your own creative ideas to them, and let God lead you deeper and deeper into His Word. You will find you can hear Him more clearly, love Him more fully, and follow Him more faithfully than ever before.

Introduction to the Leader's Guide

This introduction includes general suggestions for guiding groups through a study of *How to Hear the Living Word*. Specific help with individual sessions can be found in the appropriate sections that follow this introduction.

The most effective and efficient way to use *How to Hear the Living Word* in a small group is to have group members prepare for each session by reading the chapter *Introduction* and doing the exercises under *Tuning In* and *Pursuing* for homework. This preparation should take about an hour, and going through the study in your group will take about an hour. Suggestions in this Leader's Guide are geared to groups that do homework.

If members are not expected to do homework, you will need more than an hour in your group to do the study. You will want to begin each session by reading the *Introduction* aloud together to set the stage for the rest of the study.

If your group does homework, a good way to start each session is to ask for reactions to the *Introduction* to the literary element under discussion: What new ideas did they encounter? What questions do they have? Then invite the group to share their responses to the *Tuning In* exercise. Since this exercise is focused on personal experiences and interests, it will help the group tune in to each other as well as to the literary element they are studying.

Before you begin the *Pursuing* section, read aloud the passage or passages you will be studying. Then proceed with the questions and activities, which will get your group vitally involved in the biblical text and point them toward application in their own lives. This Leader's Guide will give you strategies for each session, suggested answers for some of the questions, and appropriate ways to close your group time—usually with prayer.

This Leader's Guide also provides suggestions for doing the *Further Exploration* exercises in a group. Even though you will probably not have time to cover these exercises in your regular small group meetings, people who attempt them on their own will be able to consult the Leader's Guide for help. And if you are

105

"lifting" selected exercises from the *Further Exploration* sections to incorporate in leadership training, this section of the Leader's Guide will be a resource for you.

GENERAL GUIDELINES FOR SMALL GROUP LEADERS

1. *Emphasize confidentiality.* The approaches in this study often call for people to respond to Scripture with personal memories or current concerns. They will not feel free to share these responses unless everyone has agreed not to let anything that is shared go beyond the group. When your group begins, ask each member to agree to this covenant of confidentiality. Periodically, remind them of that agreement.

2. *Invite but don't demand personal sharing.* On questions that ask for personal responses, assure people that they don't need to share their answers with the group; writing answers for themselves may itself be helpful enough. But because sharing difficult feelings with a group can aid in the process of healing or accountability, always give people a chance to share if they want.

3. *Make creative activities low-pressure.* Group members accustomed to a traditional discussion format may feel awkward sharing their creative responses to Scripture—pictures they have drawn, songs they have written, dramatic readings, etc. You can relieve the pressure by reassuring people that these are not supposed to be polished productions. They are simply ways to get into the passage, and when they share their responses with others, they will be helping others tune in too.

4. *Try breaking into smaller groups.* Even if your group is fairly small (8–12 people), you may want to split into smaller groups (2–5) to do some of the exercises. This saves time and allows everyone to participate more fully. Many creative projects can be done best in little groups. When people pool their ideas on a project, they will stimulate each other's imaginations and they will also feel less self-conscious about the final product. Always be sure that the smaller groups, or representatives from them, have a chance to share what they have accomplished with the whole group.

Leader's Guide for Session 1
Imagery

Note: Take appropriate note of the chapter introduction, then help your group respond to the activity in *Tuning In*. When the group is ready, conduct a discussion of the questions under *Pursuing*. Helps for some of the questions appear below.

PURSUING
Imagery in Isaiah 6:1-8

1. Encourage people to turn their imaginations loose on this passage, assuring them that it's OK if different people visualize it quite differently. The passage will gain in power and drama for all your members as people share their individual responses to it.

4. Comparing experiences, the people in your group will probably discover that God consistently works through the material world to bring about spiritual changes in us. While God came to Isaiah in a dramatic vision, He often speaks to us in more down-to-earth ways, perhaps through the beauty of nature or the words and actions of a friend. Since God knows that we live and learn through our physical bodies, He is gracious to meet us in physical ways.

5. Assure people that they may experience God in the simplest things—in the taste of a tomato from their garden or in tears they cry for a friend. As they give their answers to this question, ask them to explain why they see God's presence in the experience they have shared.

6–7. After your group has discussed Questions 6 and 7, suggest that they close with simple prayers of gratitude for the ways God has touched them and made Himself real to them lately. Encourage people to limit each prayer to one sentence, i.e., "Thank You, God, for delicious tomatoes" or "Thank You, God, for letting me share my friend's pain." That way, those who are new to praying aloud won't be intimidated by those who are more fluent in prayer.

People can start with thanks for the things they shared in Question 5, then add new ideas as they think of them.

FURTHER EXPLORATION
of Imagery in Scripture

Note: If your group has extra time, select activities from the *Further Exploration* section to enrich your time together.

Exercise 1 — Ephesians 3:16-19

A. After hearing people's responses to this question, you may want to tell them about the classic essay *My Heart, Christ's Home,* in which Bob Munger visualizes Christ taking up residence in every part of his life (including the dining room, the workshop, the rumpus room, and the upstairs closet). This essay provides a wonderful example of how the simple image of Christ dwelling in our hearts can call up a rich, imaginative response. It is available from InterVarsity Press as an inexpensive pamphlet, or as an illustratedgiftbook.

B. Encourage people to present to the group the pictures they have drawn and explain how these pictures grew out of the images from Ephesians 3:16-19. Since Paul's images are evocative, not specific, people's interpretations may vary widely.

Exercise 2 — Amos 6:1, 4-7

A. Let several people answer this question so your group can enjoy a variety of modern "translations" of Amos' images.

C. *Ruin* could apply to anything from ruined marriages to decaying inner cities to environmental pollution. As people share answers you might want to list them on a chalkboard.

Leader's Guide for Session 2
Conflict

Note: Take appropriate note of the chapter introduction, then help your group respond to the activity in *Tuning In.* When the group is ready, conduct a discussion of the questions under *Pursuing.* Helps for some of the questions appear below.

PURSUING
Conflict in Luke 9:46-50

1. Write the conflicts your group suggests on a chalkboard or flipchart. They'll probably note the conflict among the disciples over who will be the greatest, the conflict where the disciples try to stop a man driving out demons in Jesus' name, and the two clashes of Jesus with His disciples—first over their competitiveness with one another, then over their competitiveness with a perceived "outsider." After you have written these conflicts on the board, encourage the group to discuss what motives were probably behind each of the clashes. Why did the disciples act as they did? Why did Jesus act as He did?

2. Have your group try to agree on a statement of what the fundamental conflict is in this passage. They might word it something like this:

The desire to give oneself to help others who are helpless, oppressed and needy (Jesus' position)
vs.
The desire to advance one's own position and power at the expense of others (the disciples' position)

3. Divide your group into smaller groups of three or four to work on the exercises in Question 3. Each smaller group should do all five parts of the question. Give them ten minutes or so to brainstorm and agree on answers. Then gather the whole group together and have each smaller group share the names, slogans, strategies, etc. that they came up with. Create a playful atmosphere that allows people to "get into" the game.

One representative could do the presentation for each small group, but you may want to suggest before the groups start working on Question 3 that they figure out a way to involve all their members in the presentation. Perhaps they could form cheerleading squads for the opposing teams, with their cheers conveying the information called for in the exercises. Or they might have one person play the role of a sportscaster interviewing the coaches of the opposing teams.

4. Invite your group members to describe the specific circumstances where they typically find themselves gripped by a competitive spirit. Some may be competitive with a particular sibling. Others may be most competitive in school, or at work, or in social situations. If you as the leader share first, some others may feel freer to share. But don't make those who choose not to share feel uncomfortable.

5–6. These questions are designed to set up a personal dialogue between each of the group members and their Lord. They are not really intended as discussion questions. But, if someone in the group wants to reveal what he or she has written, give that opportunity.

You may want to close your study with a prayer in which you acknowledge that all people, even followers of Jesus, sometimes raise themselves up and put others down. Then invite members to pray their own silent prayers, putting their particular form of competitiveness into God's hands for healing. Finally express gratitude for Jesus' love and patience and forgiveness that is always available to us, no matter how many times we fail Him and the people He wants us to care for.

FURTHER EXPLORATION
of Conflict in Scripture

Note: If your group has extra time, select activities from the *Further Exploration* section to enrich your time together.

LEADER'S GUIDE

Exercise 1 — Psalm 73

A. The conflicts in this psalm, being mainly internal and spiritual, are not easy to pin down. After reading all the way through the psalm, read it again section by section, listening for internal struggle in each portion. The conflicts you find may include:

Trusting that God is in charge vs. feeling that the wicked are basically in control

Feeling grateful for God's blessings vs. envying the prosperity of the wicked

Focusing on the present vs. taking the long view

Feeling abandoned vs. sensing God's presence and protection

Seeing divine reality with the eyes of faith vs. believing only in what is visible and material

Self-interest vs. concern for the welfare of others

C. Resolution comes when the psalmist goes into the temple (v. 17). Somehow in that place a renewed vision of God's love and justice overwhelms his doubts and resentments. Most believers have had experiences where God simply broke through to them with His grace, making His presence and love real in the midst of doubt or disappointment. Encourage people in your group to share memories of such experiences.

D. Group members will enjoy sharing the verses that are their special favorites; they may also want to share where they keep a Scripture verse when they want to see it often.

Exercise 2 — Genesis 29:16–30:24

A. The roots of the conflict between Leah and Rachel can be found mainly in Genesis 29:16–30:24, in the differences between the two sisters, and in the ways Laban and Jacob treat them. The conflict itself is portrayed principally through the names the two women give to their children. This is an unusual literary strategy, but an effective one.

B. We are not given many details about Jacob's two wives, but we can make educated guesses about their personalities, their hopes and fears, their pleasures and hurts. Encourage your group members to use their imaginations freely on this question, feeding off of each other's ideas.

C. Your group might enjoy role-playing this question, with different people given the chance to play Leah, Rachel, and the counselor.

Leader's Guide for Session 3
Tone

TUNING IN
to Tone

Note: Beginning with the *Tuning In* exercise, this session on tone focuses on relationships that may be very painful for some people. A small group leader will be sensitive to this, allowing people to share if they want, but also allowing them to just be quiet and listen. Take appropriate note of the chapter introduction, then help your group respond to the activity in *Tuning In*. When the group is ready, conduct a discussion of the questions under *Pursuing*. Helps for some of the questions appear below.

PURSUING
Tone in Hosea 11:1-11

1. In your small group, you could go through the passage stanza by stanza (vv. 1-4, 5-7, 8-11), asking people to compare their ideas on the tones of voice and body language they imagine for each section. They may hear changes within each stanza, not just between stanzas. Assure people that it's OK if they don't all hear these verses the same way. For example, the tone of the first stanza could be predominantly sad, or wistful, or stern.

2. It can be confusing or frightening for us to meet in Scripture a God whose feelings seem so human, so passionate and unpredictable. We can see, however, that all the feelings expressed in Hosea 11 spring from God's great love for His people. If He did not care so much for them, if He had not invested so much of Himself in them, He would not feel such deep sadness and anger as well as compassion and tenderness toward them.

4-5. Each person can probably think of someone who is going in an unwise, potentially destructive direction. Questions 4 and 5 may help group members see these people more as God sees them. In your group, people can answer Question 4 in a general way without naming the person or behavior they see as foolish. In doing the rewrite of Hosea 11 for Question 5, they will be getting specific. Some members may want to read what they have written, or otherwise share the specifics of the wrong choices their loved-one is making, but you will want to re-emphasize the commitment to confidentiality which each person in the group has made.

6. Some members in your group may have felt God calling them to change their outlook or behavior toward the other person. Invite them to share their new perspective. Remind the group, however, that healing is a process and that people will be at different points in that process—some may not be ready to let go of their feelings of disappointment, anger, or despair. The Hosea passage seems to portray God Himself going through such a process before He forgave the people who had wronged Him, moving on to visualize a hopeful future for them.

Close your meeting time with a prayer of thanks that God understands all the hurts we feel and that He is the great healer. Pray for God's healing for each hurt that surfaced in the course of the discussion, and for those hurts too painful for people to express.

FURTHER EXPLORATION
of Tone in Scripture

Note: If your group has extra time, select activities from the *Further Exploration* section to enrich your time together.

Exercise 1—Acts 9:1-19

A. In your group, have four people volunteer to take the four parts in this passage, and have them read the narrative dramatically. After they have finished, others may discuss how and why they would have read certain parts differently.

B. When you focus on Jesus' words, "Saul, Saul, why are you persecuting Me?" people may hear His tone as angry, hurt, gentle,

LEADER'S GUIDE

stern, or some combination of these. Have people in turn say the words as they personally hear them, then explain why they hear them this way.

Point out to your group that this question demonstrates how our interpretation of a passage often grows out of where we ourselves are in our faith journey. As people have shared the particular tone they hear Jesus using to speak to Saul here, they have also been sharing something about how they personally see and relate to Jesus.

Exercise 2—1 Samuel 31:1-13 and 2 Samuel 1:19-27

B. This is an exercise that may be difficult for people who are not musically inclined to do on their own. Before your group begins this exercise, it will help to play brief portions of a dramatic movie soundtrack, asking people to listen for the various emotions or actions they hear reflected in the music. Then have them think in terms of appropriate background music while the 1 and 2 Samuel passages are read aloud.

Exercises like this one can be a good way to allow people who are not highly verbal but who have other kinds of gifts to make a special contribution to the group.

Leader's Guide for Session 4
Contrast

INTRODUCTION

When your group discusses reactions to the introduction, people may raise the question of how contrast differs from conflict as a literary element. Explain that *conflict* assumes an actual struggle between competing parties or forces. These parties or forces may represent the same thing. For example, when the disciples argued over who would be the greatest, they represented the same motives and values, even though they were in conflict with each other. On the other hand, *contrast* shows us two things that are opposites, but those two things may not actually clash with each other. In the Parable of the Prodigal Son, the father and his son are worlds apart in their behavior so they stand in contrast with each other, but they don't actually come into conflict—the father apparently lets his son go without protest, and he welcomes him back without reproach.

TUNING IN
to Contrast

As your group names advertisements that use contrast, you may want to list them on a chalkboard or flip chart.

Note: Take appropriate note of the chapter introduction, then help your group respond to the activity in *Tuning In*. When the group is ready, conduct a discussion of the questions under *Pursuing*. Helps for some of the questions appear below.

PURSUING
Contrast in Ephesians 2:1-10

1. Before you begin discussion, draw a copy of the blank chart for Question 1 on a chalkboard or flipchart. As people share the contrasts they have found in Ephesians 2:1-10, fill in responses on the

LEADER'S GUIDE

chart. These contrasts will probably include the following:

LIFE WITHOUT CHRIST VS.	LIFE WITH CHRIST
dead in sins (v. 1)	alive in Christ (v. 5)
objects of God's wrath (v. 3)	saved by God's grace (vv. 5, 8)
gratifying sinful desires (v. 3)	doing good works (v. 10)
following the ways of this world (v. 2)	seated with Christ in the heavenly realms (v. 6)
having Satan at work in us (v. 2)	being God's workmanship (v. 10)
rebelling against God (vv. 1-3)	carrying out God's plan (v. 10)

2. As each person in your group shares how and why one particular contrast in this passage speaks forcefully to him or her, invite others to add their own responses to that contrast. It may help if you start the discussion by sharing the contrast that moves you most deeply. For example, the picture of Satan ("the ruler of the kingdom of the air") being at work in sinners may evoke in you uneasy thoughts of a dangerous saboteur lurking close by, bent on destruction. The contrasting image of believers being "God's workmanship" may give you the exhilarating sense that God, the master craftsman, is creating and shaping your life, calling into being all your potential beauty and usefulness.

3-5. Question 3 is essentially preparation for Question 4. In your group, you may want to skip to 4 and allow plenty of time for people to share their testimonials. Remind them that these need not be polished writing; often our witness is most effective when our words are simple and spontaneous. People may choose to read what they have written, or simply speak their story.

If there is time, you may do this sharing in the whole group. But it may work best to split people into pairs so all will have a chance to share their "before and after" testimonies with one other person. Then they can do Question 5 in pairs too, giving each other affirmation that their testimony has the power to encourage other believers as well as touch the heart of an unbeliever. Then reassemble into a large group for your closing.

6. You may want to invite people in your group to pray simple sentence prayers of thanks for the changes God has made in their lives. Then you as leader can close with a prayer that God will help each person find opportunities to share with others what God has done in his or her life.

FURTHER EXPLORATION
of Contrast in Scripture

Note: If your group has extra time, select activities from the *Further Exploration* section to enrich your time together.

Exercise 1—Psalm 1

A. Encourage people to share and explain their drawings, assuring them that everyone's picture has value in helping to bring out the meaning of this psalm.

B. The psalmist's central purpose is to persuade his hearers to meditate on and live according to God's Word.

Exercise 2—Isaiah 46:1-7
A. Among the contrasts in this passage are the following:

God makes people	vs.	Idols are made by people
God rescues His people	vs.	Idols cannot even rescue themselves
God is strong and in control	vs.	Idols stoop and bow before the forces of history
God carries His people	vs.	Idols must be carried
God speaks to people	vs.	Idols cannot hear or answer when people call them

B. Possible false gods in our current society might include financial success, physical fitness and youthfulness, New Age beliefs, the power of technology to solve problems, having fun. If your group brainstorms this question, it will probably come up with many other answers. You can write these on a chalkboard or flipchart.

C. People may have different ideas about what is the most powerful false god in our culture. If you do this exercise in a group, you can let people team up with 1–3 others who choose the same idol. Then each team can write an oracle denouncing the idol they have chosen. They should be as imaginative as possible in making fun of the false god and uplifting the real God. After the teams have finished their oracles, have them share their creations with the whole group. They may want to give dramatic readings of their compositions, with all the team members participating.

Leader's Guide for Session 5
Analogy

INTRODUCTION

For the purposes of this study, the term "analogy" is used to refer to any instance where a writer takes two essentially unlike things and connects them so that the reader's imagination is stimulated to see the likenesses between them. It is not crucial for your group to understand the distinctions between simile, metaphor, and parable. The point is for them to experience how helpful it is to explore imaginatively any analogy that appears in Scripture.

TUNING IN
to Analogy

As group members share the metaphors they have written to describe their home lives or jobs, encourage them to explain what they are trying to say through their choice of metaphor. This is a good opportunity to point out that analogies are subject to misinterpretation. They can communicate truth powerfully, but they usually lack precision. That is why they leave so much room for our imaginations to work.

Note: Take appropriate note of the chapter introduction, then help your group respond to the activity in *Tuning In*. When the group is ready, conduct a discussion of the questions under *Pursuing*. Helps for some of the questions appear below.

PURSUING
Analogy in Hebrews 12:1-13

1. Christians may be like runners in a race because both:

- follow a course that has been marked out for them.
- know others are cheering them on.
- need to keep their focus on the goal and the prize that waits.

LEADER'S GUIDE

- must exercise perseverance and endure pain.
- need to throw off anything that hinders their progress.
- may grow weary and be tempted to lose heart.

2. Jesus is portrayed as the champion runner whom Christians look to for inspiration because He has already finished the race and won the prize. The description of Jesus as "author and perfecter of our faith" may suggest too that He has the role of a coach.

4–6. While Questions 4 and 5 may stir up painful memories that some group members will prefer not to share, Question 6 allows people to focus on the parts of the Hebrews passage that speak positively to them. In your group discussion you may want to skip Questions 4 and 5 and focus on Question 6. After people have answered this question, point out how wise and gracious God is to use different metaphors to make essentially the same point. He realizes that because our backgrounds and personalities are different, we may be able to relate better to some word pictures than to others.

7–8. Invite people to share the "pep talks" they have written and explain why the metaphor they chose is "tailor-made" for their particular friend. You could close your group with a prayer thanking God for designing His Word so that it's power can touch each unique person. Thank Him specifically for the Hebrews passage on running the race of faith, and pray that its pictures will comfort those in the group who are in the midst of painful times, yet challenge any who have grown comfortable and complacent in faith.

FURTHER EXPLORATION
of Analogy in Scripture

Note: If your group has extra time, select activities from the *Further Exploration* section to enrich your time together.

Exercise 1 — **Philippians 2:14-16**
A. Following are ways that joyful Christians may be similar to stars:

- they contrast with the darkness around them.
- they are beautiful and appealing.
- they give light that can guide others.
- they don't shine alone, but in concert with other Christians.

C–D. People have the opportunity here to speak of their weaknesses with the group, but in a light, even humorous way. Perhaps someone might say, "Rather than shining like a star, I get in a grumpy mood that hangs like a big black cloud over all my relationships." The value of defining our own negative behavior in some kind of memorable word picture is that we get a clearer sense of the ugliness of that behavior in contrast to the beautiful picture of shining stars. Also, we will be more apt to recognize and correct the negative behavior when it rears its ugly head in the future.

Exercise 2—Matthew 7:1-5

A–B. Try splitting your group up into smaller groups of 4 or 5 for this activity. Give the groups time to discuss the point of the parable and to develop and rehearse their contemporary sketches. (Twenty minutes should be enough time.) Then bring the groups together and have each group perform its comedy sketch, so others can see how each skit finds a different way to illustrate the main point of the parable—that we often judge others for the very sins we ourselves commit.

Leader's Guide for Session 6
Repetition

Note: Take appropriate note of the chapter introduction, then help your group respond to the activity in *Tuning In*. When the group is ready, conduct a discussion of each question under *Pursuing*. Helps for some of the questions appear below.

PURSUING
Repetition in Daniel 3:1-30

1. Ask someone to volunteer to read Daniel 3:1-30 aloud before you begin your discussion. The more dramatically that person can read, the better.

2. Clearly the king is asking people to worship an idol. The repetitions underline the foolishness of people *falling down* before a "god" that has been *set up* by a man.

3. The repetitions of the king's commands give us a picture of a pompous, self-important ruler who likes to order people around and revel in ostentatious ceremonies. In contrast to the rather humorous sing-song repetition surrounding the king is the straightforward speech of the three Jews. Their words give us a picture of men who are not proud or argumentative. Instead they delight in serving God, and their deep confidence in Him makes them courageous and totally honest.

5. By repeating the *three* names so often up to verse 23, the writer of the story heightens the surprise that both Nebuchadnezzar and the reader feel when the fourth person appears in the furnace in verses 24-25. The lesson of the story, that God Himself is always present to save those who put their faith in Him, jumps out at us more clearly.

7. Some people may be willing to share the dialogue they have written in a group, but don't pressure them. You may want to ask, instead, how doing this exercise worked for people. Did they find writing a dialogue with God hard or easy? Did they gain new insights into themselves or God by doing this? Do they think this would be a good kind of exercise to do regularly in their quiet times?

If one or two people are willing to share their dialogues, they could read these as a closing prayer. Or you could close by emphasizing how God was with Shadrach, Meshach, and Abednego in the fiery furnace, then inviting people to pray sentence prayers in this format: "Thank You, Lord, that You are with me in . . . ."

FURTHER EXPLORATION
of Repetition in Scripture

Note: If your group has extra time, select activities from the *Further Exploration* section to enrich your time together.

Exercise 1 — Ecclesiastes 1:2-11

A. Examples of repetition people may find include:

- The word *meaningless* is repeated in verse 2.
- Four kinds of cycles are described in verses 4-7: generations coming and going, the sun rising and setting and rising again, the wind returning on its course, water moving from streams to the sea and back to streams again.
- Four kinds of human desires (vv. 3, 8, 11) are never fulfilled: man's endless labor brings no lasting gain; the eye never has its fill of seeing; the ear never has its fill of hearing; men's achievements will not be remembered.
- Words like *all* and *everything* are repeated to emphasize that nothing escapes the meaninglessness the poet sees.

B. The theme of this passage is that there is no progress, only repetition, and there is no fulfillment, only desire. All the repetitions underscore this theme of meaninglessness.

C. People may share varied reactions to this bleak poem. Some will find it so depressing that they wonder why it is included in the Bible. It is probably there to remind us how the world must look to a person who doesn't believe in God, only in what he can see with his senses or achieve by his own efforts.

Many people will enjoy the artistic use of imagery and the powerful, almost hypnotic rhythm of the repetitions in this poem. Even ugly ideas can give us pleasure when they are presented effectively, when the form perfectly mirrors the contents as it does here.

Exercise 2—2 Timothy 2:14-26

A. Repetition is not always artistically done (as it was in the Daniel and Ecclesiastes passages). But even writers who express themselves in more prosaic ways tend to reveal their special concerns by the use of repetition.

In 2 Timothy 2:14-26, Paul seems preoccupied with words, used either rightly (to convey truth, to call on God, to gently instruct) or wrongly (for quarreling, godless chatter, false teaching). The main problem facing Timothy seems to be combating false teaching and foolish arguments.

B. To do this activity in a group, split into smaller groups of 3 or 4. Explain that even though Paul does not repeat his ideas in a particularly rhythmical way in this passage, those ideas will be easier for us to absorb and remember if we put them in a musical format. After the smaller groups have written their song titles and choruses, have them regather to share them with the whole group.

Leader's Guide for Session 7
Omission

Note: Take appropriate note of the chapter introduction, then help your group respond to the activity in *Tuning In*. When the group is ready, conduct a discussion of the questions under *Pursuing*. Helps for some of the questions appear below.

PURSUING
Omission in Luke 19:1-10

2–4. These questions call for imaginative guesswork. As leader, your role is to help group members turn their imaginations loose.

Even if they have written out answers for homework, try to encourage a brainstorming atmosphere. Assure people that all their ideas, even "far out" ones, are welcome. Members may contradict each other, or even themselves, but in the process they will stimulate one another's imaginations and help deepen their experience of the Bible passage. You don't need to question guesses that seem "off-base." In the course of discussion, your group will probably challenge any ideas that are not consistent with what we know about Jesus and about the role of tax collectors in first-century Palestine.

5. We can be pretty certain Zaccheus was lost morally (he probably cheated others to get rich), relationally (his neighbors hated him), and spiritually (in choosing to be a tax collector for the Romans, he'd known he was cutting himself off from the Jewish faith). We might also surmise that he felt lost vocationally—perhaps his hunger to see Jesus was an indication that he no longer found satisfaction in his lucrative profession. We are not sure of all that Jesus may have said or done when He visited Zaccheus, but the fact that this man, God's Messiah, defied every rule and prejudice of Jewish society and extended His love to Zaccheus had a transforming effect on the tax collector. He was saved morally (he repented of his cheating), relationally (in Jesus he found a perfect friend), spiritually (Jesus assured him that he too was a son of

LEADER'S GUIDE

Abraham, one of God's chosen people), and vocationally (he now saw a satisfying way to use all the money he had made — to help the poor). Your group may point out these or other answers.

6. The response of the townspeople to Jesus' invitation to Zaccheus indicates that most of them were lost in their own self-righteousness, in their complacency over being God's chosen people, and in their willingness to assume that God shared their own hatred for sinners like Zaccheus. Their rigid attitudes made them resistant to the salvation Jesus offered. But probably Jesus' public demonstration of attention and respect for Zaccheus was designed, at least in part, to call into question all their self-satisfaction and judgment and to show them how different God's priorities were from their own.

7–9. These three questions encourage people to allow the story of Zaccheus to touch and challenge them personally. Before group members share their answers to these questions, you might ask your group this more general question: "How has using your imagination to fill in holes in this account helped fill in holes in your understanding of Jesus? How has it filled holes in your understanding of yourself?"

After inviting any who want to share their responses to questions 7–9, close your group with prayers around the theme of "lostness." Encourage each person to write down one or more sentence prayers either thanking Jesus for how He has rescued them from being lost (i.e., "Jesus, thank You for coming to me when I was lost in _____.") or asking for His saving grace in a current situation where they feel lost (i.e., "Lord, I'm searching for _____ and I've lost my way. Please help me."). Then invite people to pray their prayers, either silently or aloud.

FURTHER EXPLORATION
of Omission in Scripture

Note: If your group has extra time, select activities from the *Further Exploration* section to enrich your time together.

HOW TO HEAR THE LIVING WORD

Exercise 1 — Acts 16:16-25
A–B. One way to approach this exercise in your group would be to assign different teams to develop interviews with the various people in the Acts account. One team could interview Paul and the slave owner, a second team could interview the slave girl and one of Paul's companions who witnessed the exorcism, and a third team could interview a magistrate and one of the Romans in the crowd. Each team could think of three or four questions to ask each person and then discuss possible answers the people might give. Then one member of the team could act as interviewer and others could play the interviewees in order to present the team's ideas to the whole group.

Following are sample questions that an interviewer might want to ask of each person listed below:

Paul: Why did you drive the spirit out of the slave girl? What gives you the power to drive out spirits? How do you feel about the way you've been treated today?
Slave Owner: Do you believe that what your slave girl said about these men being servants of the Most High God is true? Do you really think they present a danger to our town and its citizens?
Slave Girl: How do you feel about Paul and what he did for you? What do you think you will you do now, since you cannot predict the future anymore? What do you think about this Jesus Christ Paul talks about?
Magistrate: What crimes have Paul and Silas committed? Why didn't you question them and listen to their side of the story?
Paul's Companion: Why do you follow this man Paul? Why did your group come to Philippi in the first place? Do you think Paul should have driven the spirit out of the girl, or left her alone?
Roman in the Crowd: How did these two men react when they were accused and beaten? Do you think they are harmless crackpots, or dangerous criminals?

Exercise 2 — Genesis 22:1-18
B. In a group, you might have people pair off, then assign each pair to work on a different element in the film version of Abraham's sacrifice of Isaac. One pair might visualize the setting, an-

LEADER'S GUIDE

other the lighting, a third the sound effects and music. After these teams have come together and shared their ideas, the group as a whole could discuss the question of whether or not more dialogue would contribute to the impact of the story and, if so, what dialogue they would add.

C. The eternal truths people find in this story may include:

- God wants us to surrender all we are and have to Him and to obey Him completely.
- If we trust God, He will provide all that we need.
- We can have faith that God will carry out His plans and keep His promises, even when we cannot see how He is doing this.

Leader's Guide for Session 8
Hyperbole

Note: Take appropriate note of the chapter introduction, then help your group respond to the activity in *Tuning In*. When the group is ready, conduct a discussion of each question under *Pursuing*. Helps for some of the questions appear below.

PURSUING
Hyperbole in Psalm 18

2. Exaggerated pictures of David's prowess appear in verses 29, 33-34, 36-38, and 42. Group members may enjoy comparing the wording from their different versions. They will discover that some translations tend to tone down hyperbolic language while others accentuate it. For example, in the *Good News Bible* verse 36 reads, "You have kept me from being captured and I have never fallen." In the *New Jerusalem Bible,* the same verse reads, "You give me the strides of a giant, give me ankles that never weaken."

Group members will enjoy seeing the cartoons others have drawn. If some people haven't actually drawn cartoons, encourage them to describe for the group how they visualize David's actions being portrayed in a comic book.

3–4. God's strength is often pictured as something solid, massive, and protective. He is a rock, a fortress, a stronghold, a refuge, a shield. God's very essence is strength. David's strength, on the other hand, is seen in terms not of what he is but of what he can do—scaling a wall, bending a bow of bronze, crushing his enemies, and beating them as fine as dust. David's strength is a moment-by-moment strength that is given by God when he needs it. God has the only solid, permanent strength that can be depended on. Thus David opens the psalm by acknowledging that God is his strength.

5–7. Point out to your group that as they share their responses to these three questions, they will be experiencing three different ways Christians who are feeling weak or defeated can find

LEADER'S GUIDE

strength. Question 5 gives them the encouragement of hearing how God has worked in other people's lives. Question 6 asks them to look for comfort in Scripture. And Question 7 shows them a way to find strength by visualizing who God is and how He will work for them in the future.

If two or three people have written psalms they are willing to share, you might let them read these as your closing prayer. Or invite people to pray sentence prayers acknowledging and praising God for His strength (i.e., "Lord, You are my rock." "Thank You, Father, for keeping Your strong arms around me.").

FURTHER EXPLORATION
of Hyperbole in Scripture

Note: If your group has extra time, select activities from the *Further Exploration* section to enrich your times together.

Exercise 1 — 1 Corinthians 13:1-3

A. Speaking with the *tongues of angels,* fathoming *all* mysteries and *all* knowledge, having the faith to *move mountains,* giving *all* I possess to the poor, *giving my life as a martyr* — these are very exalted and in most cases exaggerated pictures of what people are actually capable of doing.

Exercise 2 — Micah 7:2-4

A–B. In your group it might be fun to begin by instructing members to line up along an imaginary spectrum on the floor, with those who see themselves as "hyperbolic" at one end and those who see themselves as "restrained" at the other. Let them rearrange themselves and each other until they are satisfied with the order. Then ask everyone to share how they would react to hearing Micah's denunciations spoken about our society today. This exercise will demonstrate that how we react to figurative language like hyperbole in Scripture depends in large part on our different personalities.

C. People who tend to see things in exaggerated, black-and-white terms as Micah does may get angry at what angers God, may be decisive, and may be spurred to effective action. But they may also be judgmental, rash, or so pessimistic that they despair of doing any good.

Restrained, cautious people, on the other hand, may be more balanced and less judgmental. They can see various sides of an issue or situation, so they can serve as mediators and peacemakers. But they may also be indecisive, slow to act, and too tolerant of things that God abhors.

Help your group appreciate and respect each other's differences. Point out that just as God gives people different gifts that complement each other in the church, so He gives people different responses and perspectives on the Bible and on life, and uses these differences to do His work in the world.

Leader's Guide for Session 9
Poetic Justice

Note: Take appropriate note of the chapter introduction, then help your group respond to the activity in *Tuning In*. When the group is ready, conduct a discussion of the questions under *Pursuing*. Helps for some of the questions appear below.

PURSUING
Poetic Justice in Revelation 17, 18, and 19

1. This is a long Scripture selection. The assignment to jot emotional responses in the margin will help people keep their attention focused on the passage. In group discussion there won't be time for everyone to trace all their emotional reactions to the passage, but you may want to ask each member to share his or her predominant reaction.

2. The sins of Babylon include seducing men and nations and making them drunk, blaspheming, indulging herself with luxuries, persecuting the saints who bear testimony to Jesus, boasting, and asserting her independence from God. People may also find a reference to enslaving people in 18:13, and a reference to practicing magic in 18:23.

The metaphor of "adultery" captures Babylon's unfaithfulness to God, which is evidenced in her blasphemy, her boasting, her dependence on material wealth for satisfaction, her practice of magic, and her persecution of God's people. The metaphor of "prostitution" fits with the fact that Babylon seduces men and nations into sin, and her seductions are principally commercial in nature, growing out of her greed.

3. This question gives group members a chance to discuss how they feel about the injustices they see in this world. Encourage them to share their feelings honestly. Perhaps seeing people enjoy undeserved success or endure undeserved suffering causes some of them to doubt God's existence or to feel angry at Him. Reas-

HOW TO HEAR THE LIVING WORD

sure them that these are legitimate feelings and that the writers of the Psalms frequently express similar feelings.

4. Revelation 18:2 and 21-23 paint the picture of a deserted, dead place. Apparently all that is left of Babylon is an unrecognizable heap of rubble. What a comedown for the once great city that was the thriving center of so much activity, the magnet for merchants from all over the world. Where once there was music, and craftsmanship, and business, and light, and love, now there is only silence and darkness, demons and evil spirits, and the kind of "unclean" birds that feed on dead things. The true emptiness and evil of Babylon have been exposed.

Revelation 18:5-8 uses the picture of Babylon being forced to drink terrible things from her own cup. As she became intoxicated with the blood of the saints she tortured (see 17:4-6), now Babylon will suffer a double portion of torment herself. All the abominations she visited on others will be visited on her. The plagues of death and mourning and famine which she thought could never touch her will now overtake her. (Since she was such a glutton, being plagued with famine is a particularly fitting fate for her.) She who thought she was so mighty is now totally at the mercy of God's might.

5. The startling contrasts between Revelation 18 and Revelation 19 appeal strongly to our senses and emotions. Cries of lament seem to fade away into ominous silence in Revelation 18, in sharp contrast to the shouts of praise that burst forth in Revelation 19. In Chapter 18 the luxuries of Babylon piled up in long lists convey a sense of obscene hedonism, but we then learn that all these luxuries have vanished. Instead, in Chapter 19 we see simple, pure, beautiful pictures of the fine linen (white and clean) that the saints will wear and of the wedding supper with the Lamb that they will enjoy.

  a. Your group as a whole might work out an effective dramatic reading of Revelation 18:1–19:9. Different group members could take different parts—John as narrator, the angels in heaven who pronounce doom on Babylon, the woeful kings and merchants and sea captains who mourn her downfall, the

LEADER'S GUIDE

multitude in heaven who praise God, the angels who pronounce a final blessing on believers.

b. If people have done collages at home, display them for the group and invite people to respond to what they see in them.

c. If people have created posters of phrases from Revelation 17–19, invite their creators to present them to the group in any way they choose. Perhaps they will simply display them, or read them like a poem, or explain why they chose the phrases they did and arranged them as they did.

6. Invite any group members who are struggling with current unfair circumstances to share them with the group. You may want to stop and pray for each one as they share particular struggles. After they have spoken, have all members explain why they find particular verses in Revelation 17–19 especially encouraging and inspiring.

Instead of a closing prayer, you could have your whole group read in unison (or even shout in unison) the words in quotation marks from Revelation 19:1-9. They will be cheering for God, joining the heavenly chorus in affirming His perfect justice which will triumph in the end.

FURTHER EXPLORATION
of Poetic Justice in Scripture

Note: If your group has extra time, select activities from the *Further Exploration* section to enrich your time together.

Exercise 1 – Matthew 18:23-35
A. A summary of the acts in this parable might read like this:

ACT I	*The master demands payment of a huge debt.*
	Servant 1 cannot repay.
	The master decides to sell the servant and his family.
	Servant 1 pleads for mercy.
	The master forgives the debt.
ACT II	*Servant 1 demands payment of a small debt.*
	Servant 2 cannot repay the debt and pleads for mercy.

HOW TO HEAR THE LIVING WORD

Servant 1 does not forgive, but throws Servant 2 in prison.

ACT III   *The master throws Servant 1 in prison.*

C. The lesson of this parable might be stated: "Forgive those who sin against you," or "Forgive others, as God has forgiven you," or simply, "Forgive others."

Exercise 2—Genesis 25:24-28; 27:1-35; 37:1-35

A. Commentators often note that Jacob seems to get caught in traps similar to the ones he has set for others. In Jacob's early days his father Isaac favored his brother Esau over him, but he circumvented his father's favoritism by deceiving him with a cruel hoax, putting on Esau's clothes and using the skin of slain goats to convince blind Isaac to give him the blessing instead of his brother Esau. Decades later Jacob favored his son Joseph, which caused resentment among Jacob's other sons. They sold Joseph into slavery, then deceived their father with a cruel hoax, convincing him that his favorite son was dead by taking Joseph's coat and staining it with the blood of a slain goat. Jacob visited the same kind of hurtful favoritism on his sons that Isaac had visited on him, and consequently his sons subjected him to the same kind of cruel deception he had made his father suffer. The fact that clothing and goats play a role in each account heightens the sense of poetic justice.

C. Some believers are uncomfortable with the picture of a God who punishes personally, so they tend to emphasize the natural cause-and-effect aspect of justice, theorizing that people bring their own suffering on themselves. Other believers prefer to see every part of life as coming directly from God's hand, feeling that it is better to be disciplined by a personal God who can also love and forgive and redeem than by some impersonal law of cause and effect.

The Bible actually presents both perspectives on poetic justice—sometimes picturing wicked people falling into their own traps, but other times showing an angry God personally involved in punishing sinners. Apparently both pictures are true.

Leader's Guide for Session 10
Paradox

INTRODUCTION

The exercises in this session deal with tensions in Scripture around the topics of sanctification, prayer, and women's roles. Some people may object that one or more of these topics is not truly paradoxical. Perhaps they have already worked out a satisfactory resolution of the question in their own minds, or perhaps they come from a doctrinal background that has settled the issue for them. Remind these people that ongoing debates within the church on these topics indicate that contradictory views can legitimately arise out of the relevant biblical texts. Encourage them to open themselves to the possibility of paradox around these issues.

After reading the Introduction, some members of your group may be anxious to discuss the question of eternal security and debate the correct interpretation of the two passages from John. You should cut this discussion short, or postpone it, so you'll be sure to have plenty of time for the *Tuning In* exercise and the study in Ephesians 1 and 5.

Note: Take appropriate note of the chapter introduction, then help your group respond to the activity in *Tuning In*. When the group is ready, conduct a discussion of the questions under *Pursuing*. Helps for some of the questions appear below.

PURSUING
Paradox in Ephesians 1:3-23; 5:1-20

1. Among the verbs describing what God does for believers: He *blesses* (v. 3), *chooses* (v. 4), *predestines* (v. 5), *gives* grace, wisdom, and understanding (vv. 6-8), *makes known* His will (v. 9), *works out* His purposes (v. 11), *calls* them to hope (v. 18). All these verbs are active.

The verbs that describe the believer's role (see especially v. 11) are almost all passive: believers are *adopted* (v. 5), *chosen* and

HOW TO HEAR THE LIVING WORD

predestined (v. 11), *included* and *marked* with the seal of the Holy Spirit (v. 13) and *enlightened* (v. 18). Even the active verbs assigned to believers imply something they have been given—they *have* redemption because Christ died for them (v. 7); they *hear* truth (v. 13) and *know* Christ because God gives them the Spirit of wisdom and revelation (v. 17). Perhaps the only truly active verb applied to believers is the verb "believe" (v. 13). Help your group members to discover these insights as they examine the text.

2. Ephesians 5:1-20 is full of commands to believers to make choices, refraining from some behaviors and embracing others. In verses 3-7 Christians are told to avoid immorality, impurity, greed, foolish talk, and being deceived, among other things. Rather, they are to be imitators of God and live a life of love (vv. 1-2). Paul commands them, in verses 8-20, to find out what pleases God, expose deeds of darkness, make the most of every opportunity to do God's will, be filled with the Spirit, and give thanks to God, among other things.

In Ephesians 5:1-20, Paul gives only passing mention to what God, through Christ, does for believers (see vv. 1-2, 8-9, 15). God loves us as His children. Christ modeled love for us in His sacrificial death. In Christ we are given light so that we can see what is evil, and we are made "light" so that we can live as children of light, producing the fruits of goodness, righteousness, and truth.

3. Ephesians 1 shows God doing all the work of salvation, with believers as passive recipients of His grace, wisdom, and power. Ephesians 5 urges us to be active participants in our spiritual growth. As members of your group try to find the balance between these two truths, they will probably recognize that it is not a question of God doing a certain percentage of the work of sanctification and us doing the rest. Instead, believers live in a mysterious tension, depending completely on God for their growth, yet at the same time accepting their responsibility to choose and strive to live in God's love and light, filled with His Spirit.

4–6. Questions 4 and 5 point to the wonderful blessings that flow from both truths in the sanctification paradox. Believers who ac-

LEADER'S GUIDE

tively trust God for their growth live with a sense of peace, expectancy, confidence, and gratitude that frees them to serve God and love others. Believers who acknowledge their God-given responsibility to choose and strive to be like Christ are energized by the exciting knowledge that they are God's fellow workers in the kingdom, that He wants their help and is pleased by their efforts.

Questions 4 and 5 also explore the dangers of forgetting that both God and the believer play an important role in sanctification. Those who focus on God's role instead of their own responsibility may let their freedom in Christ turn into license. They may become lazy, fail to use the gifts God gives them, and fall into temptation. On the other hand, those who focus on their own effort and discipline instead of God's grace may become either guilt-ridden Christians who stand in judgment of themselves or self-righteous Pharisees who stand in judgment of others.

People's answers to Questions 4 and 5 are closely related to their responses to Question 6. In your group you may want to skip discussing 4 and 5 and instead stage a debate around Question 6. Invite people to join one of two teams, depending on whether they believe most of the Christians they know need to trust God more for their spiritual growth or need to increase their own effort and discipline in their walk with the Lord. With the teams facing each other, invite representatives of each team to try to persuade their opponents to their point of view. People can change sides if they change their minds. You won't resolve the question with this debate, but you will have a lively discussion that illuminates why the paradoxical truths the Bible teaches about sanctification need to be held in tension in the Christian life.

7–8. Before people share their answers to these questions, you can point out that there are times in our lives when we may need to hear one side of a paradox more than another. In times of stress or pressure to perform, God may want us to learn to rest more in His grace. In times of ease or complacency, He may want to stretch us with a sense of our need for greater discipline. There is always the danger, however, that we will hear the side of the paradox that is more comfortable for us, not the side that God wants us to hear. That is why it is good to try to enter into both sides of the truth that a paradox teaches.

You can close your group by reading Ephesians 6:10-18. This passage about putting on the armor of God incorporates the tension between depending on God and taking responsibility for our own Christian walk. You may want to change the passage into a prayer: "Father, help us be strong in Your mighty power. Help us put on the full armor of God so we can take our stand against the devil's schemes...."

FURTHER EXPLORATION
of Paradox in Scripture

Note: If your group has extra time, select activities from the *Further Exploration* section to enrich your time together.

Exercise 1—**Paradoxes surrounding prayer**
A. When we pray, should we always say to God, "Not my will, Lord, but Thine," realizing that what we want may not be what God desires? Or should we pray with childlike trust, believing that our heavenly Father wants to and will give us whatever we ask of Him? The Bible seems to teach both approaches.

Exercise 2—**Paradoxes surrounding women's roles**
A–B. Genesis 1 presents woman as man's equal, standing in exactly the same relation to God as he. Both sexes are to be fruitful and subdue the earth and rule over all other living creatures. Genesis 2 shows woman being created after man and out of man, designed by God to "be a helper suitable for him." There is tension here: do men and women have equal standing and identical roles in the created order? Or are women to be subject to men with a different role in the created order?

A similar tension shows up in I Corinthians 11:3-12. Paul clearly advocates a hierarchy, with Christ the head of man, man the head of woman. Different head coverings and hair styles are proper for the different positions of man and woman. Yet Paul assumes that in the church both men and women will pray and prophesy—a radical indication of equality compared to the silent role women played in Jewish public worship. When Paul alludes to creation, he seems to become particularly tangled up in the tension between views of equality or hierarchy. "For man did not come from woman, but woman from man"; Paul says, "neither was man created for woman, but woman for man." Yet one verse later he contends, "In the Lord, however, woman is not independent of man, nor is man independent of woman. For as woman came from man, so also man is born of woman. But everything comes from God."

Leader's Guide for Session 11
Dramatic Irony

Note: Take appropriate note of the chapter introduction, then help your group respond to the activity in *Tuning In*. When the group is ready, conduct a discussion of each question under *Pursuing*. Helps for some of the questions appear below.

PURSUING
Dramatic Irony in Luke 24:1-35

1. In your group you may want to take some time to talk about what it would have been like to be among the followers of Jesus that first Easter morning. Encourage some members to put themselves in the place of the women, while others are assigned to empathize with the men. Then people can share what they think they would have felt during the events in verses 1-11, and why they would have either believed or doubted.

2. Your group should discover dramatic irony evident in:

- Verse 18, with Cleopas asking Jesus if He is the only One who doesn't know what has happened to Jesus of Nazareth.
- Verse 19, where the two men use the past tense to refer to the very person they are talking to.
- Verses 21-24, where the two men themselves state reasons they should believe in the Resurrection, yet they still think Jesus is dead.
- Verses 26-27, when Jesus Himself explains to the men the Scriptures that pointed to Him, yet they still don't catch on to who this "stranger" is.

6. The stages the men go through in this account might include:

- The Resurrection seems like nonsense at first hearing.
- They talk out all they have seen and heard, trying to make sense of it.

LEADER'S GUIDE

- They listen as Jesus interprets the Scriptures for them.
- Moved by Jesus' teaching, they ask for His continued presence with them.
- They recognize Jesus as their Savior.
- They witness to others about their risen Lord.

7–8. Both these questions give group members a chance to share how Christ has worked in their own lives—acknowledging that faith has sometimes been a struggle but recognizing that the Lord was present in that struggle. After those who want to have shared their answers to Questions 7 and 8, close your group time with prayer. You might return to the theme of a surprise party, inviting members to thank God for specific instances in their lives when He has surprised them with His presence, power, and gifts.

FURTHER EXPLORATION
of Dramatic Irony in Scripture

Note: If your group has extra time, select activities from the *Further Exploration* section to enrich your time together.

Exercise 1a—2 Samuel 11:1-27
A. Invite people to present their charts to the group and summarize what these charts show about the personalities of David, Uriah, and Joab. Below are some traits and behaviors people may have discovered in the three men, with verses where we see these operating:

- *David:* shirks his duty (v. 1), uses his power to exploit another and indulge his own desires (vv. 3-4), speaks words that are hypocritical and slick (vv. 7-8, 25), is willing to corrupt another to save himself from shame (vv. 13-15), is ruthless and cowardly (v. 15).
- *Uriah:* is self-controlled (v. 9), motivated by principle, not self-gratification (vv. 9, 13), straightforward (v. 11), dedicated to his soldierly duties (v. 11), obedient to authority when it does not go against his principles (v. 12).
- *Joab:* follows the king's orders without question (v. 16), uses soldiers as expendable pawns (v. 17), does what he knows is unwise militarily to please the king (vv. 19-21), is devious (v. 21).

It will be interesting to compare the various ways your group members found to display the different personalities of these three men on a chart.

B. Uriah chooses not to go home and sleep with his wife, thus obstructing David's plan to cover up his sin. Even David's urging (v. 10) and plotting (v. 13) cannot get Uriah to go home. Finally, anxious to get back to his soldierly duties at the front, Uriah carries to General Joab a letter containing the orders for his own murder.

C. In verse 11 when Uriah states his principles to the king, he unwittingly indicts the king's own sins. Uriah is aghast at the idea of enjoying the comforts of home and sleeping with Bathsheba while his fellow soldiers are at war, yet this is exactly what David has been doing—enjoying the comforts of home and sleeping with Bathsheba, when he himself should have been at war with his army.

Exercise 1b—**2 Samuel 12:1-13**
B. The two men of the parable are clearly David and Uriah. David is the wealthy one who, though he has plenty of wives (sheep) of his own, decides to take Uriah's "little ewe lamb," his only wife whom he loves dearly. David is so spoiled by the power his position gives him that he uses Bathsheba to gratify a momentary desire without even thinking how this may hurt her and her husband. Uriah, who is in a much more humble position, does not take his blessings and responsibilities lightly. He cherishes Bathsheba and cares for her—just as we saw him cherishing and being careful of his role as a soldier in chapter 11.

D. Because Uriah, a noble soldier, is the unsuspecting victim of a scheme by the sinful and conniving David in chapter 11, the effect of the dramatic irony is tragic. We are heartsick when we see that Uriah's good behavior will lead to his death. This isn't the way life should work, and it makes us particularly angry at David. As king he should be rewarding a man like Uriah, but instead David uses his power to exploit him, putting his own gratification and self-protection before godly principles.

In chapter 12, the sinner David is the victim of the trap laid for him by God's prophet Nathan. Because the sentence David unwittingly pronounces on himself is exactly what he deserves, the effect of this dramatic irony is comic. We have great satisfaction in seeing the selfish trickster get tricked. But we also cheer at the success of Nathan's scheme because it is a godly scheme that actually calls forth the best in David, his inherent sense of fair play and compassion. This story ends with David repenting of his sin and experiencing God's forgiveness in verse 13.

Leader's Guide for Session 12
Echoes

INTRODUCTION

Echoes are closely related to repetition. In fact, they are a kind of repetition and have the same power to point us to what is important in God's Word. The difference between repetition and what I call "echoes" is that repetition occurs in a clearly defined literary unit — a single poem or passage or book — that we are apt to read in one sitting, whereas echoes reverberate across a wide expanse of Scripture. They are similar pictures or themes that surface in a variety of books, usually beginning in the Old Testament and carrying into the New. While any careful reader can recognize repetition in a single text, it is only as we familiarize ourselves with large parts of Scripture in both the Old and New Testaments that we can appreciate the power of the echoes that the divine Author has built into His Word and His actions over long centuries of biblical history.

Note: Take appropriate note of the chapter introduction, then help your group respond to the activity in *Tuning In*. When the group is ready, conduct a discussion of the questions under *Pursuing*. Helps for some of the questions appear below.

PURSUING
Echoes of the Marriage between God and His People

1. The prophets see the marriage relationship between God and Israel originating far in the past and stretching ahead into a promised but not yet fulfilled future. There are variations in the way they view the drama, but its basic elements can be outlined in four acts:

ACT I   *God chooses Israel to be His beloved bride, makes a covenant with her, cares for her, protects her, and makes her prosper.*

LEADER'S GUIDE

ACT II Israel is unfaithful to God. Forgetting all He has done for her, she flouts His laws, squanders His good gifts, and prostitutes herself by worshiping idols.

ACT III God punishes Israel for her unfaithfulness. Because she has put her trust in other nations and their gods, God abandons her to these foreign "lovers" who turn on her, abuse her, and humiliate her.

ACT IV God, still in love with His people, restores Israel as His wife and once again brings her glory and honor.

Help your group members discuss their various outlines.

2. Encourage several people to reflect aloud on their own histories with God.

3. People's answers may vary on where Jesus fits into the Old Testament marriage drama. Since He is God, come in the flesh to the nation of Israel to reconcile sinners to Himself and establish a new, intimate love relationship with them, He can be seen as the embodiment of Act IV. But it could be argued that His life and death is actually ACT V because He took the divine-human marriage relationship in a new direction. He did not reinstate the old relationship between God and Israel, but called as His bride a new people, the church, which included Gentiles as well as Jews.

Responses to this question may be colored by people's theology, particularly if they have strong views on the correct interpretation of Old Testament prophecy and how the church fits into this prophecy. As group leader, discourage arguments over doctrinal issues. Instead, point out that when the Old Testament prophets described Act IV in the marriage drama, their beautiful word pictures probably foreshadowed more than one coming reality. They seem to have pointed in part to a restoration of the Jewish exiles to their homeland before the time of Christ. They also pointed to Christ's first coming and to His second coming. The prophets did not see clearly or precisely the full scope of God's plan, but in their marriage metaphors they did capture a sense of the depths of

God's forgiving love and the lengths He would go to to establish a new closeness with sinful people.

4. Again, you are looking for people's impressions, not definitive answers. The bride in these passages is, variously, the local church at Corinth, the church universal, the gathered saints, or the New Jerusalem. She is a gift being prepared for Christ, and when He comes again, she will be waiting for Him like a bride, radiant and beautiful, pure and righteous. But the Ephesians passage suggests that Jesus is already married to His bride and it is He who is making her pure and beautiful, first by dying for her and then by continuing to nurture her with His love.

Before your group moves on to Question 5, you may want to review with them how listening for echoes of the theme of marriage between God and His people in various parts of Scripture has impacted them. How did reading the Old Testament prophetic passages add to the meaning of the bridegroom and bride images in the New Testament? How did reading the passages in the Epistles and Revelation enhance the significance of the bridegroom images in the Gospels? How did focusing on the divine-human marriage theme in the New Testament heighten their appreciation of the prophets' visions?

5. After those who want to have shared their answers to this personal question, suggest that the group as a whole develop "marriage vows" to be spoken between Christ and the believer. Ask first for the words Christ as husband would speak, and write ideas on the chalkboard. Then ask for ideas on the vows the bride should say, and write those. After the group has polished the vows to its satisfaction, use them to close your meeting, with one person reciting the words of Christ, then everyone responding with the vows of the bride. Begin, "Jesus says...."

FURTHER EXPLORATION
of Echoes in Scripture

Note: If your group has extra time, select activities from the *Further Exploration* section to enrich your time together.

LEADER'S GUIDE

Exercise 1 — **Echoes of drinking the cup God gives**
B–C. The Old Testament passages show that the image of the cup God gives is an image of judgment. The cup is full of God's wrath, and He makes those who are wicked drink that cup. Thus, when Jesus applied this image to His coming crucifixion, He signified that by dying He would be taking on Himself the punishment that God would otherwise visit on sinners. He would actually have to experience the wrath of His Father. Furthermore, since the Old Testament associated the image of the cup of God's wrath with horrible pictures of bloodshed, humiliation, helplessness, madness, and utter ruin, we realize that Jesus knew full well, and had reason to fear, the depths of suffering He would endure in the Crucifixion.

Exercise 2 — **Echoes of God's preference in choosing people**
A–B. The thread running through God's choices in the Old Testament is that He seems to consistently prefer the younger or weaker candidate to carry out His plans. In the New Testament we see the same pattern. Jesus said we must become like children to enter the Kingdom. He Himself came as a baby, and the first people God chose to hear the good news of His coming were lowly shepherds. Jesus in His death displayed surprising weakness and humility, not the overwhelming strength one would expect God's Messiah to exercise. And He called on His disciples to become like the youngest, to become ones who serve.

Checklist

LEARNING STRATEGIES THAT MINE THE LITERARY RICHES OF SCRIPTURE

WAYS TO ENTER INTO A PASSAGE IMAGINATIVELY

- Write down your spontaneous reactions to the passage. (See pages 28, 50, 58, 66, 69.)
- Ask what the narrative makes you see, hear, smell, feel, taste. (See page 15.)
- Imagine what people in the passage were thinking and feeling. (See pages 15, 54, 86, 109.)
- Meditate on a word picture and the ways it appeals to your senses and feelings. (See pages 17, 34–35, 42.)
- Ask of an analogy, "How many ways can I think of that the two things being compared here are similar?" (See pages 41, 43, 69, 89.)
- Develop character sketches based on the words and behavior people in the passage exhibit. (See page 25.)
- Imagine dialogue or prayers that people in the passage would say. (See pages 55, 58.)
- Note in the margin the tones, expressions, and gestures that might accompany the words in the text. (See page 28.)
- Think out how you would film the narrative. (See pages 58–59.)
- Imagine background music for a passage. (See page 31.)

WAYS TO CONNECT THE PASSAGE TO YOUR OWN LIFE AND WORLD

- Translate the imagery into modern terms. (See pages 18, 65.)
- Think of a contemporary situation that teaches or illustrates the same things this passage does. (See pages 44, 65, 70.)
- Put yourself in the passage and ask, "What would I have thought, felt, said, done?" (See pages 54–55 and 142.)
- Ask how you display the same trait or traits modeled by one of the people or represented by one of the word pictures in the

CHECKLIST

passage? (See pages 22, 24, 44, 56.)
- Identify the qualities demonstrated in the passage that you wish were more evident in yourself. (See page 56.)
- Ask at what point the passage touches you most deeply. (See pages 18, 24, 34–35, 64.)
- Rewrite the passage so it speaks specifically to yourself or someone you know. (See pages 23, 29, 43–44, 65.)

ANALYTICAL ACTIVITIES

- Make a list. (See pages 23, 38, 49–50, 63, 69, 78–79.)
- Devise a chart. (See pages 34, 88 and 143–144.)
- Underline or circle elements in the passage. (See page 47.)
- Focus on verbs. (See page 78.)
- See both sides of an issue. (See pages 66, 74, 79–80, 82.)
- Define the stages in a narrative or the acts in a biblical drama. (See pages 72–73, 87, 93–94.)
- State concisely the central conflict, the problem addressed, or the main lesson taught in a passage. (See pages 21, 50, 73.)

CREATIVE WRITING ACTIVITIES

- Think up slogans. (See page 21.)
- Develop a commercial or testimonial. (See page 35.)
- Write your own oracle, psalm, etc. (See pages 38, 64, and 119.)
- Dialogue with God (or with Jesus) writing out a verbal exchange between Him and yourself. (See page 23, 49, 95.)
- Compose song lyrics. (See page 50.)

ART ACTIVITIES

- Draw a picture. (See pages 17, 37.)
- Sketch a cartoon or comic strip. (See page 62.)
- Make a collage. (See page 71.)
- Create a poster or plaque. (See pages 65, 71.)
- Arrange Bible verses or phrases on a page so their meaning is highlighted. (See page 71.)

HOW TO HEAR THE LIVING WORD

SPEAKING AND DRAMA ACTIVITIES

- Stage a debate. (See page 139.)
- Write and perform a skit. (See pages 44 and 122.)
- Do a dramatic reading of a passage. (See pages 30, 71, and 134–135.)
- Interview a Bible personality. (See pages 56–58 and 128.)
- Role play. (See pages 25 and 112.)

MISCELLANEOUS ACTIVITIES

- Place yourself on a spectrum. (See pages 66 and 131.)
- Create hypothetical teams to represent different sides of a conflict, contrast, or paradox. (See pages 21–22 and 109–110.)